QUEST IN PARADISE

David Attenborough's new book describes his two remarkable expeditions to the South Seas in search of people and their primitive way of life, although it was the lure of seeing birds of paradise in their natural surroundings that drew him into the heart of primitive New Guinea. With Charles Lagus he set out from the Wahgi Valley and trekked for many days along the narrow jungle path into the Jimi Valley. They encountered stone-axe makers, richly adorned tribesmen, and a race of pygmies, and here they achieved their main objective and watched the fabled dance of the birds of paradise.

On his return David Attenborough was determined to explore the islands farther to the East, and luck was with him, for last year he received an invitation to visit Tonga. On his way there he went to the islands of the New Hebrides, saw the sensational land-divers on the island of Pentecost and learned about the god John Frum and the extraordinary 'cargo' cult on Tanna; in Fiji he was captivated by the native peoples, watched fire-walking and the calling of turtles, and took part in the ceremonial fishing of a sacred lake. Finally in Tonga he met Queen Salote and filmed the Royal Kava Ceremony which few Europeans have been privileged to witness.

David Attenborough's previous books have established him as a leading author, and this new work, describing so vividly and amusingly his experience among the strange tribes of New Guinea and the gay and friendly South Sea Islanders, will add greatly to his reputation as a daring explorer, an acute observer, and a brilliant raconteur.

QUEST
IN PARADISE

DAVID ATTENBOROUGH

UNABRIDGED

PAN BOOKS LTD : LONDON

First published 1960 by the Lutterworth Press.
This edition published 1963 by Pan Books Ltd.,
8 Headfort Place, London S.W.1

Printed in Great Britain by Richard Clay and Company, Ltd.,
Bungay, Suffolk

Contents

PART ONE
THE BIRDS OF PARADISE

PART TWO
THE PEOPLE OF PARADISE

ILLUSTRATIONS
IN PHOTOGRAVURE

between pages 96 *and* 97

Acknowledgements

To travel is to make friends and the pleasure of doing so is not the least of the joys of a journey. During the two trips described in this book, we were particularly fortunate in the number of people who befriended us and the unstinting and imaginative ways in which they gave their help. Some of them appear by name in the pages that follow and I hope that part of our debt to them will be apparent. Among the very many others who are not mentioned are: in New Guinea – Mr and Mrs Frank Balogh, Mr Frank Buscumbe, Mr Alan Ferguson, Mr Ron Focken, Mr Barry Osborne, Mr and Mrs H. S. Sibary, and Mr and Mrs John Womersley; in the New Hebrides – Mr and Mrs Reece Discombe, Mr Tom Mitchell, Mr and Mrs John Rennie, Mr and Mrs Cyril Williams, and Mr Keith Woodward; in Fiji – Mr Josua Bogi, Mr Jack Hackett, Mr George Rawnsley, Mr Christopher Venning, and Mr Rob Wright; and in Tonga, Mr J. McComber and the Hon. Vaea. To them all I am extremely grateful.

Once again I must record my thanks to the British Broadcasting Corporation and to Mr Leonard Miall for the mounting of the expeditions and to Mr Michael Foxell of the Lutterworth Press for his patience and encouragement during the writing of them.

DAVID ATTENBOROUGH

Richmond, Surrey
September 1960

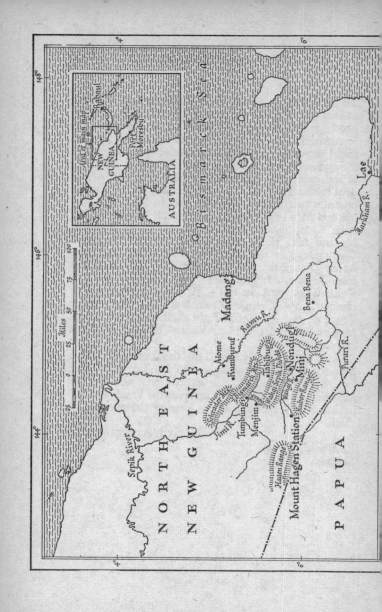

PART ONE

THE BIRDS OF PARADISE

CHAPTER ONE
Fowle of the Sunne

AMONG THE marvels brought ashore from the ship *Victoria* when she reached Spain on September 6, 1522, after having completed the first journey around the world, were five bird skins. Their feathers and in particular the gauzy plumes sprouting from their sides were of a matchless splendour and magnificence and quite unlike anything that had been seen before. Two of them had been given to Magellan, the leader of the expedition, by the King of Batchian, an island in the Moluccas, as a gift for the King of Spain. Pigafetti, the chronicler of the expedition, recorded the gift and wrote that 'These birds are as large as thrushes; they have small heads, long beaks, legs slender like a writing pen and a span in length. They have no wings but instead of them, long feathers of different colours like plumes: their tail is like that of a thrush. They never fly except when the wind blows. They told us that these birds come from the terrestrial Paradise, and they call them bolon dinata, that is divine birds.'

Thus these gorgeous creatures became known as Birds of Paradise. They were the first recorded specimens ever to come to Europe. Pigafetti's account of them was relatively unsensational. No doubt they had been shorn of their wings by the native skinners in order to emphasize the glory of their plumes. But their breathtaking beauty, their extreme rarity, their association with the 'terrestrial Paradise' invested the birds with an aura of mystery and magic, and soon there were stories about them as fantastic as their beauty. Johannes Huygen van Linschoten, describing his own voyage in the Moluccas seventy years later, wrote that 'In these Islands onlie is found the bird which the Portingales call passeros de sol, that is Fowle of the Sunne, the Italians call it Manu codiatas and the Latinists, Paradiseas, and by us called Paradice-birdes, for ye beauty of their feathers which passe al other birdes; these birdes are never seene alive, but being dead they fall on the Ilands: they flie, as it is said alwaies into the sunne, and keep themselves continually in the ayre, without lighting on the earth for they have neither feet nor wings, but onlie head and body and for the most part tayle.'

The lack of legs described by Linschoten is easily explained, for even today natives habitually remove the legs of the birds to make the task of skinning easier. The fact that Pigafetti had stated that birds of paradise possessed legs was either conveniently forgotten or else forcefully contradicted by later writers in their anxiety to sustain the romance of the stories surrounding the birds. However, Linschoten's descriptions of their mode of life posed a number of problems to the thoughtful naturalist. If the birds were always in flight, how did they nest and incubate their eggs, and what did they eat? Soon answers were devised, answers that were as impossible as the fancies they sought to rationalize.

One writer described how 'there is in the back of the male a certain cavity, in which the female, whose belly is also hollow, lays her eggs and so by the help of both cavities, they are sitten upon and hatched.' Another, after explaining that the birds, during their perpetual flight, fed only on dew and air, added that instead of a stomach and intestines, which would have been useless to so extraordinary a feeder, the cavity of the abdomen is filled with fat. A third, hoping to add credibility to the story of their feetlessness, and having noticed that pairs of curling wiry quills are found among the plumes of some species wrote that 'They sit not upon the ground, but hang upon boughs by strings or feathers which they have and so rest themselves, like flies or aierie things.'

Even two hundred years after the first skins had come to Europe, the exact identity of the birds' home, the 'terrestrial Paradise' was still unknown. It was not until the eighteenth century that it was discovered that they lived in New Guinea and its offshore islands. When European naturalists saw the living birds in their natural surroundings for the first time, most of the myths surrounding them were dispelled. Nevertheless, the air of romance which surrounded the birds ever since Pigafetti's time has never quite been forgotten and when Carl Linnaeus, the great Swedish naturalist, gave a scientific name to the species most likely to have been described by Pigafetti, he called it *Paradisea apoda,* the Legless Bird of Paradise.

But the scientific discoveries of the last two hundred years have revealed that the true facts about the birds of paradise are almost as fantastic as the earlier legends, for the birds possess some of the most splendid and improbable feather adornments to be found in the entire bird world. Over fifty different species are now recognized which differ widely in shape and size. Some, like *Paradisea apoda,* have cascades of filigree plumes growing from beneath their wings, others bear huge iridescent shields of feathers on their chests. Some have long, glossy black tails glinting shades of purple, in others the tail feathers are reduced to wires. Wilson's Bird is bald with a bright blue scalp, the King of Saxony's Bird has two head plumes twice the length of its body, each adorned with enamel-like plates of pale pearly blue. The biggest are the size of crows; the smallest, the red King Bird of Paradise, is little larger than a robin. The birds of paradise, in fact, are alike only in that their plumage is of almost unbelievable extravagance and they indulge in ecstatic courtship dances during which they display their glorious plumes to drab hens.

Such beautiful and romantic creatures were surely worth going thousands of miles to see, and for years I had been obsessed by the thought of doing so. The London Zoo had not exhibited specimens for several years, and at the time that I was pondering on an expedition to go in search of them, it possessed none at all. Furthermore, no film had ever been shown, in this country at least, of the wild birds performing their display dances. I decided that I would go to New Guinea, make an attempt to film them, and bring some back alive to London.

New Guinea is immense. It is the largest non-continental island in the world, over a thousand miles from end to end. It is ridged by chains of mountains as high as the Alps, the upper slopes of which are mantled not with snowfields and glaciers, but with forests of giant trees hung with sodden moss. Between these ranges run huge valleys clogged with jungle, many of them virtually unexplored. Towards the coast spread vast mosquito-ridden swamps hundreds of square miles in extent.

Politically the island is divided into two almost equal parts: the western half is governed by Holland and the eastern by Australia. The Australian territory is also divided administratively, for the south-eastern quadrant, Papua, is an Australian possession but the north-eastern is held under the trusteeship of the United Nations. In the highlands of this last territory, close to the centre of the whole island and just north

13

of the Papuan border, lies an upland valley which has become famous among ornithologists, for here, at a small settlement called Nondugl, an Australian millionaire-philanthropist, Sir Edward Hallstrom, has established an Experimental Farm and Fauna Station. He has built great aviaries which now contain more birds of paradise than all the zoos of the world put together, and living there, at the time we were planning our trip, was one of the greatest of all animal collectors and an expert on the Paradisea, Fred Shaw Mayer. Nondugl, therefore was the ideal place for us to visit, if we could get permission to do so.

Sir Edward has for many years been a friend and benefactor of the London Zoo, and when I wrote to him and told him of our ambitions he replied suggesting that we should use the station as our base for our four-month expedition.

CHAPTER TWO

The People of the Wahgi

CHARLES LAGUS and I had already tackled three animal collecting and filming trips in the tropics together. As we sat in an airliner being rushed eastwards towards our fourth, both of us were immersed in the worries which unfailingly trouble us at the beginning of a new journey – he mentally checking his photographic equipment, fearful that he had left some vital item behind, I trying to anticipate all the bureaucratic obstacles with which we should be faced before we reached Nondugl and attempting to reassure myself that we had anticipated and prepared for most of them.

Within three days we had reached Australia. From Sydney we flew northwards to New Guinea. In Lae, on the north-east coast of the island, we disembarked from a comfortable four-engined aircraft and boarded a less luxurious plane which each week flies up with supplies to the Wahgi valley in the central highlands.

We sat on aluminium, shelf-like seats which had been set up along half the length of one of the sides. In front of us lay a long mound of cargo running the length of the cabin and lashed with ropes to rings in the deck. It contained mail bags, armchairs, massive cast-iron parts of a diesel engine, cardboard boxes full of day-old chicks, a great number of loaves of bread and, somewhere among it all, sixteen pieces of our own baggage and equipment.

Our fellow passengers were seven half-naked Papuans who sat rigid and tense, with tight lips and set expressions, staring with unseeing eyes at the pile of cargo stacked a few inches in front of them. For some of them at least, this was their first flight – before we took off I had had to show them how to fasten their seat belts – and their brown skins glistened with little beads of perspiration.

Rain spattered against the small windows, its sound drowned by the roar of the engines. I could see nothing outside but greyness. The plane rocked and shuddered as we rose higher and higher over invisible mountains. I shivered slightly for it was cold and my skin was still clammy with the sweat which had poured from me in the muggy heat of Lae.

The plane climbed steadily until the grey cloud outside began to disintegrate into racing wraiths of mist. Suddenly the cabin brightened as though an electric light had been switched on. I looked out of one of the windows. The sun was sparkling on the polished, quivering wings of the aircraft. Several miles away, dark peaks, like islands, jutted through the immobile billows of clouds. Soon, rents appeared in the white shroud beneath us, each an oddly unreal vignette revealing sometimes the serpentine twist of a silver river, sometimes a few minute huts, but most often, featureless green corduroy. These glimpses of the land beneath grew in size and number until at last they fitted together into a continuous picture of range after range of razor-backed hills rising in succession, some thickly forested, some naked but for uniform brown grass. One after the other, their crests passed beneath us until abruptly they dropped and we were no longer flying over savage escarpments but along a wide green valley. This was the Wahgi.

Less than thirty years ago, the existence of this valley was not only unknown but totally unsuspected. The first people to find a clue to its presence were two Australian gold prospectors, who in 1933 were travelling down the Purari River on the southern slopes of the huge mountain ranges which were then supposed to occupy the whole of the centre of New Guinea. No Europeans had been there before and as the Australians worked their way down the Purari, stopping every now and then to wash the gravels from the river-bed in the hope of finding grains of gold, they arrived at a point where

15

another broad river flowed into the Purari from the mountains to the west. Floating in this river, the prospectors saw corpses. The bodies were of big men, of a type the Australians did not recognize. Some bore arrow wounds, and one had a deep gash in the skull which must have been made with some weapon like an axe. Whatever else was to be found among the headwaters of this new river, there must certainly be an unknown and warlike population.

Three years later, one of the prospectors, Michael Leahy, was again working in the unexplored country at the head of the Purari. He climbed a small hill and looked west. Above the wall of mountains that formed the skyline hung a bank of clouds. To the north and the south there were high cumulus, typical of the clouds which so often crown the mountain peaks of New Guinea; but in the middle, they were lighter and thinner. Leahy reasoned that this difference must imply a difference in the shape of the land beneath them, and further that the central clouds were similar to those which form above grassland. Recalling the corpses he had seen three years earlier which must have come from the country beneath the clouds, he decided that the curtain of mountains in front of him concealed a large unknown valley. He determined then that he would be the first to enter it.

Next year, with his twenty-one-year-old brother, Dan, and Jim Taylor, a Government officer, he climbed the mountain wall. He reached the top, looked over and saw, as he had hoped he would, a wide fertile valley. The next day, as the party marched into it, they were met by a wonderful and strange people, wearing magnificent head-dresses of bird of paradise plumes. These people had never seen white men before, nor had they heard of the existence of the sea. They had no knowledge of metal and were armed with huge stone war-axes. Not only had the explorers discovered a new valley, which was to become known as the Wahgi, but they had also discovered a new people.

The Leahys made several more journeys into the valley, but before many other Europeans were able to go there, to explore in more detail, the Second World War broke out. A few men travelled through the valley either escaping from or chasing the Japanese, but it was only after 1945 that any real settlement took place there. Yet in this very short space of time, the Wahgi valley has been transformed. Government stations are now scattered along its length. There is quite a large European population who are farming, raising cattle and sheep, or planting coffee; dirt roads link station to station and, perhaps most important of all, there is a string of airstrips along its length, for the Wahgi, like most of the interior of New Guinea, has been colonized primarily from the air. The Leahys' first action after their initial pioneering journeys had been to find sites which could be cleared so that planes might land to bring them stores and support. Later settlers, having received grants of land, adopted the same methods. In no other country has this technique been used with such skill, verve and audacity and, as a result of it, central New Guinea has been opened up at an extraordinary speed.

One of these landing grounds was built to service the experimental farm at Nondugl. Our plane dipped low over the station buildings. A tiny truck emerged from one of the sheds and moved slowly down the thin red line which scarred the landscape connecting the houses to the airstrip. We landed bumpily and, as Charles and I climbed stiffly out, the truck raced round the bend, on to the grassy strip and squealed to a halt beneath the plane's wing. Two men jumped out. One, a stocky, burly man wearing a broad-brimmed, sweat-stained hat and khaki overalls, introduced himself as Frank Pemble-Smith, the manager of the station. The other, an older, thinner man, was Fred Shaw Mayer.

Together we unloaded our goods from the plane. Frank swore mildly when he discovered that some spare parts for his farm machinery were not in the cargo and spent a few minutes exchanging gossip with the pilot. Then the plane's engines restarted, it roared down the strip, heaved itself into the air and headed for the next station which, in flying time, was only four minutes away. Frank arranged for his Papuan station hands to load our gear on to the trailer of a tractor which had been waiting close by, and then he whirled us off in his truck to meet his wife and have tea in his house.

Frank's bungalow stood among neatly clipped lawns and red earth paths. In front of it stretched an ornamental lake, around it lay flower beds planted with vivid gladioli, and above it nodded a tall clump of creaking feathery bamboo. Beyond the lawns I could see stables, workshops and garages and, beyond these, paddocks full of sheep and lambs. Southwards the house looked across the wide Wahgi valley to the Kubor mountains, indigo blue in the heat haze. Northwards, and relatively close to it, rose the high forested mountain wall

17

which divides the Wahgi from the still largely unexplored area beyond, the Jimi River valley. The sun shone brilliantly and the air was tingling fresh, a joy to breathe after the soporific, moisture-laden atmosphere of the coast.

As we ate Sue Pemble-Smith's scones, each plastered with thick cream from Nondugl's dairy herd, I could see standing motionless outside the startling figure of a tall, heavily-bearded and semi-naked man. His brown arms and hairy chest had been blackened by soot and his face was painted with dots and stripes of red, yellow, and green. His waist was encircled by a broad stiff cummerbund, made from woven fibre, over the front of which hung a narrow length of woolly fabric reaching down to his shins. Behind, like a bustle, he had tucked a bushy spray of leaves. He was decked with a wealth of pearl-shell jewellery: a belt of small pieces hung from a string around his waist; a huge pearly breastplate was suspended from a cord round his neck; a broad crescent encircled his chin, partially concealing his beard; and he had inserted a long slender sickle, cut from the rim of a pearl-shell, through the pierced septum of his nose. His most dazzling and resplendent personal adornment, however, was neither his pearl-shells nor his paint, but his gigantic feather head-dress. It contained the plumes from at least thirty individual birds of paradise belonging to five different species. Ruby, emerald, velvet black and enamel blue, these marvellous feathers formed a crown of unbelievable splendour.

His magnificence seemed the more startling because of his setting, for he was standing on a freshly mown lawn and had, for his background, the wire-netting fence of a tennis court. Parked by his side was a bright red tractor. I found myself looking at him as I would view a circus exhibit or a tourist attraction. Yet when I glanced higher up at the wild mountains behind, it was the tennis court, the tractor and the china teacup from which I was drinking which struck the jarring, intrusive note. It was I who was in the circus, and the man outside, together with thousands of his compatriots in the forests beyond, who were the audience.

Frank saw me staring. 'That,' he said, 'is the local headman – the *luluai*. His name is Garai and he's one of the wealthiest and most amiable of all the local boys. I told him that you two fellows were coming to look for birds of paradise and I expect he's waiting about to be the first one to tackle you in case there's any trade to be done.'

When we had finished tea, we went out to meet him. He shook hands with us enthusiastically, but with the indefinable awkwardness of someone to whom the action is an unfamiliar one, and grinned broadly, exposing a perfect set of massive white teeth.

'Arpi-noon, masta,' he said.

'Arpi-noon,' I replied, pleased to be able to use almost the only phrase of pidgin English I knew. Unfortunately, I was unable to add anything else, for you cannot speak pidgin merely by adding 'um' or 'ee' to the end of normal English words. It is a language in its own right, with its own syntax, grammar and vocabulary. It was created comparatively recently, largely by the people of New Guinea themselves, to enable them to communicate, and therefore to trade, not only with the white foreigners who came to their country but also with one another, for in New Guinea over one hundred different native languages are spoken.

Pidgin has taken its vocabulary from many sources. Some words come from Malay – *susu* for milk, and *binatang*, which, when I had learned it in Indonesia a year earlier, meant animal but which here has its meaning narrowed to insect. There are also German words, for this part of New Guinea was once a German colony – *raus*, clear out; *mark*, which is still often used to mean a shilling; and *kiap* which seems to be a corruption of *kapitan* and is now used to mean a government officer. There are also, of course, many Melanesian words. But the bulk of the vocabulary is derived from English. In the transition from one language to another many of these words are run together and have had their consonants softened to suit the native tongue so that, when written with their official spelling, a little imagination is needed to divine their oorigin – *kisim*, give him, *pluwa*, the floor, *solwara*, the sea, *motaka*, a car, for instance. This spelling can be so confusing that in such pidgin conversations that I give here, I have adopted a less accurate but more easily understandable version. Some words have taken on a new meaning – *stop* means to be present not to finish, and *fella* is added to many words to indicate an entity. Some expressions have had their meaning so transformed that it is unwise to try to improvise recklessly lest some of your remarks take on a highly indelicate and totally unintended meaning, and the whole language is usually salted with so many full-blooded Australian expletives

19

that a normal conversation can make a genteel and unprepared Englishwoman blench in horror.

Frank told Garai why we had come to Nondugl.

'You lookim,' he said. 'Dis two-fella masta e stop long Nondugl. E like findim all kind pidgin, na all kind binatang. Garai, you e savvy place belong altogether pidgin, na you e showim dis place, na masta e givim Garai plenty mark.'

Garai grinned and nodded enthusiastically. I mentioned to Frank that we were also hoping to make a film about the local people and their ceremonies.

'Suppose you fella like makim big-fella sing-sing,' Frank continued. 'Dis two-fella masta e givim picture long dis-fella sing-sing.'

Garai replied with a torrent of pidgin, spoken so rapidly and with such an unfamiliar intonation that I could not understand. Frank translated.

'Tomorrow night,' he said, 'a courtship ceremony called a *kanana* is going to be held down in Garai's settlement. Do you want to go?'

It was our turn to nod enthusiastically.

'Na two-fella masta e like talk "thank you too much",' said Frank. 'Behind, long dark e come up tomorrow, e like come place belong you an lookim dis-fella kanana.'

The next night Garai arrived at Frank's bungalow to escort us to the kanana as he had promised. We followed him through banana groves and past thickets of bamboo, creaking in the breeze. The air was cold and vibrant with insect noise. It was near midnight but we had no need of our torches to help us find our way for the moon was full and the sky clear.

After a quarter of an hour, we reached Garai's hamlet surrounded by casuarina and banana trees. He led us past several low, circular, thatched huts. Through chinks between the stakes which formed the walls came the glimmer of fires and the subdued murmur of conversation. We stopped in front of a hut which was larger than the rest and of a different shape. It was about forty feet long and through the thatch at either end projected the ends of a pair of poles. One of each pair was shaped as a female symbol, the other as a male. Banana trees loomed black above it, silhouettes against the starry sky.

Garai pointed to the low entrance.

'Na you two-fella masta go lookim, one-fella somet'ing e stop inside,' he said.

We crawled in on our hands and knees. Immediately I was

assailed by stifling heat and choking, acrid smoke. I could see nothing for my eyes were smarting so much that I was unable to open them. When, after a few seconds, I forced myself to do so, I was still able to see very little for tears welled out of them, blinding me.

Stooping, with my hand across my smarting eyes, I clumsily picked my way through a tangle of squatting figures until I found a vacant space at the far end of the hut where I could sit down. As soon as I did so, to my relief and surprise, my eyes stopped watering for the smoke was hanging only in the rafters and beneath the air was clear. I looked around.

The smoke came from a wood fire which smouldered in the centre of the earth floor, its flames providing the only light in the hut. By its side, his back against one of the soot-blackened centre poles, sat an old bearded man. Apart from ourselves, he was the only man in the hut; the people among whom I had stumbled as I entered were all young and buxom girls. They sat in two long lines facing inwards and were watching me curiously, giggling among themselves.

'Masta i come makim kanana?' said one of them, a rhetorical question which was answered by shrieks of laughter.

None of the girls flaunted a magnificent head-dress like that of Garai's which we had seen on our first day, for the low roof of the hut would have made it impractical to wear them. Instead they wore small skull caps, crocheted from the wool of tree kangaroos or opossums and bound on to their heads with circlets of glittering green beetles enclosed in a framework of split cane. Their faces were painted with dots and stripes of many colours, each girl having her own design which had been dictated not by any ritual compulsion but by her own personal fancy. Most wore necklaces of beads or crescents of pearl-shell either round their necks or through their noses, and all had the wide waist-band of woven orchid fibre that denotes an unmarried girl. Their bodies had been smeared with pig-fat and soot, and glistened in the dim, flickering firelight.

No sooner had we found a place to sit than a line of men, headed by a grinning Garai, crawled in. They sat themselves in between the girls, but facing the walls of the hut. They, like the girls, were splendidly decorated and painted but, in addition, most had stuck leaves and pieces of fern in their skull caps. They were not, however, all young. Some had bushy beards; some, like Garai, we knew to be already married, but, although the kanana is a love-making ritual, this was

21

not improper, for the Wahgi society is a polygamous one. These men had all been specially and personally invited to the ceremony and many had come from hamlets many miles away.

For a few minutes, while people settled themselves, there was gossip and laughter. Then a single voice began hesitatingly to sing. One by one, other voices joined in until everyone was singing a slow chant. As the song gained momentum, the men and the girls began to sway their bodies from side to side, rolling their heads as they did so. The cadences of the chant were repeated hypnotically, and the swaying bodies came closer together, each man inclining his torso towards the girl sitting facing him on his right. Closer they came, the droning chant mounting to a climax until, with eyes shut, the pairs of faces met nose to nose, forehead to forehead. Ecstatically each couple rolled their heads from cheekbone to cheekbone in a delirium of sensuous delight.

A few dancers broke away from one another quite quickly, and looked abstractedly around the hut, ignoring their partners. Most of them, however, continued swaying, lost in their pleasure, their faces joined.

The song died and at last everyone separated and began to chatter. One of the girls lit a long cigarette made from newspaper and drew in lazy lungfuls of smoke. Each man crawled around the girl with whom he had danced and sat down by the side of the next girl in line so that everyone, as in a Paul Jones, had changed partners. Once again the chant started, the dancers began to sway, and once again as the climax of the song was reached, faces met together and rocked from cheek to cheek.

We sat watching for hours. It became so hot that I took off my shirt. The fire smouldered lower until all I could see of the dancers was a glint of an oiled body or the moving shape of a white owl's wing which one of the men wore in his skull cap.

One of the dim figures close to me let out a deep chuckle. It was Garai.

'Eh lookim,' he whispered, and pointed to a couple who had broken away from the main dance and were sitting in the shadows with their arms around one another, the girl's legs resting over one of the man's thighs.

'Im e carry-leg,' said Garai.

During the kanana ceremony itself, custom forbids the dancers to touch one another except with their faces. The old

22

man sitting in the centre was there to enforce the rule. But a girl can indicate by the enthusiasm with which she rubs noses whether she likes her partner or not. If a pair are mutually attracted then they may leave the line of dancers and 'carry-leg', and such friendships made during the kananas often ripen into marriage. It was indeed like a Saturday night dance in England.

By three o'clock, the ranks of the dancers had thinned considerably. We crawled out of the hut and into the cold night.

*   *   *

The next day, Garai, looking very tired but having lost none of his cheerful ebullience, came to us bursting with delight and pride. He had discovered from one of the men at the kanana an item of news which he was sure would interest us.

'Me savvy place belong pidgin. Dis-fella kind, im e workim lik-lik house long ground,' he said, giving little nods of enthusiasm by jerking his head back and raising his eyebrows.

In spite of the flamboyant gestures of his hands with which he tried to indicate the size and peculiar shape of the bird's 'little house', we were unsure exactly what it was he was describing. Nonetheless he would have been woefully disappointed if we had not taken notice of his great news, so we picked up our cameras and followed him as he set off at a trot along a narrow muddy path that led out of the station towards the hills.

Charles and I panted behind him; neither of us was yet in condition for route marches at such a pace. We crossed several muddy gorges, waded across two streams, forced our way through great areas of tall, dusty kunai grass which scratched our arms painfully, and at last, about two miles from Nondugl, reached some low but very thick bush which had sprung up on the site of a long abandoned plantation. We had to duck low and use our bush knives to clear a passage. At last Garai stopped. Panting and pouring sweat, we caught up with him.

'Lookim,' he said excitedly, his eyes sparkling.

He was pointing to a small bare space among the ferns and grass that grew beneath the viciously spiked boughs of a bush. In it, I saw an extraordinary construction of twigs and dried grass stems. It consisted of three parallel walls each about a foot high. The two channels between them were neatly floored with interlaced twigs. The central wall, thicker than the two which flanked it, was grooved across its middle by a deep notch so that, viewed from above, the notch and the two channels formed a letter H. Channels and notch were scattered with bright blue berries. Garai had brought us to the display ground of a bower bird.

I grinned back at Garai. 'Im good-fella house too much,' I said.

Bower birds are for the most part drab creatures and none of them possesses the superb plumes that birds of paradise flaunt in front of their hens. Instead their displays are carried out with these bright berries which the cock bird collects and hoards in his bower. Every day he comes to the bower to re-arrange his treasures, to discard faded or shrivelled ornaments and add new ones.

Garai plucked a bright red flower from a bush near by and dropped it in the bower.

'Dis-fella pidgin e come,' he explained. 'E lookim dis t'ing. E raus im. Behind, masta e lookim. Flower e gon. Masta savvy pidgin e come sing-sing dis-fella house.'

I was excited, for if we discovered by the means that Garai was suggesting that the bower was still used, we might be able to get some fascinating film of the bird bringing berries. Charles was more practical.

'No good,' he said. 'It's not that this delightful house be-long pidgin is too lik-lik, but that this-fella bush is so wretchedly dense that you couldn't possibly see the nest from more than three feet away; and if we build a hide as close as that the bird will never return.'

We examined the possibility of clearing a channel of bush to give us a view of the nest from a more distant hide, but Charles was right: the bower was unfilmable. Reluctantly we left it and pushed our way out through the scrub.

We had not been walking for more than ten minutes when I heard a distant drumming and singing. We crossed one of the kunai patches and saw coming down the path towards us a spectacular procession. At its head strode several men resplendent in enormous feather head-dresses and carrying long three-pronged spears. But they were merely the heralds of an even more impressive sight, for behind them came a man carrying aloft on top of a pole a giant standard, three feet across, ablaze with gorgeous colour. It was a banner of woven cane and grass hung with a dozen shining pearl-shells, mats sewn with valuable cowrie shells, tiaras of scarlet parrot feathers, and around its rim thirty or forty sets of bird of paradise plumes. Behind the standard bearer walked more men, women and children each of whom carried pieces of smoked pig-flesh – a flank, a spine, a leg, a head or entrails wrapped up in leaves. One man held a drum which he thumped to accompany his yells as the whole party advanced towards us down the path through the kunai.

We stood to one side to let them pass and Garai told me what was happening. The men had come from the hills on the other side of the Wahgi valley and were on their way to collect a bride. The arrangements for the marriage had been made long before, when representatives from both families had met and agreed between them the exact price in feathers, shells and pigs that the groom must pay for his bride. The price was high and to have amassed it all would have taken years, so the bride's parents had agreed that the marriage could come into effect on payment of a substantial part of the price, provided that regular instalments were made afterwards until the full sum had been paid off. The bridegroom had then made long and arduous trips into the forest hunting birds of paradise for their plumes. Some of the pearl-shells he had borrowed from relations, some he had earned by working for one of the older and wealthier men in the village. At last he had enough to serve as a deposit and two days ago he and other members of his family had set out on the long march to the bride's hamlet. With them they took the bride-price – the pearl-shells, the pig-meat and the paradise plumes, which were carefully wrapped in protective folders of dried leaves stiffened with split cane lest during the journey their filigree beauty should be marred. Last night the party had slept in the forest. When they arose at dawn, they had constructed the huge banner and decked it with the shells and the feathers so that the munificence and fine quality of the bride-price should be seen by all. Now they were nearing the bride's home which lay only another hour's walk away. Garai spoke to one of the warriors who followed in the banner's wake and asked for permission for us to follow them.

The banner bobbed and swayed ahead of us and the vociferous chant of the party echoed across the sun-baked valley. Garai pointed out a small grassy spur running down from the mountains and crowned with a little clump of casuarinas.

'Im, im,' he said, stabbing the air vehemently with his finger and clutching my forearm. 'Im place belong meri.'

Meri was one of my more recently acquired pidgin words. It means woman or any female creature and is often spelt *mary* as though, like so many other pidgin words, it was originally English. I had already constructed in my mind a fictitious derivation for it: one of the first English traders to settle on the coast brought his wife with him, her name was Mary and the local people quite naturally used it to signify their own women. Unfortunately this is wholly false. It seems likely that *meri* is not of European origin at all but comes from a local language, for early travellers, writing long before pidgin English developed, have quoted it.

We followed behind the wedding party for mile after mile. Eventually we emerged from the bush and began toiling up the long grassy spur. A hundred yards from the trees that surrounded the bride's hut, we had to climb over a savagely spiked fence that formed a defensive palisade, a relic of the warlike period that had ended only a few years ago. On the other side of it, the standard-bearer was waiting to allow stragglers to catch up with him. Then, when all had assembled and smartened themselves up, the procession slowly and in a dignified manner advanced towards the bride's hut.

The bride and her family were sitting in the small clearing in front of their hut awaiting the banner's arrival. I was unsure as to which was the bride until Garai pointed her out to me. She was the most unlikely looking member of the group for such a role, for not only was she comparatively old, but she was also holding a young baby. She was, Garai explained, a widow.

The standard was planted firmly in the ground in the middle of the clearing, and the bride and her family got to their feet to welcome the visitors formally. They embraced, putting their arms around one another's shoulders and waists with an air of slightly forced affability not unlike the handshakes between comparative strangers who find themselves newly related by law at a European wedding reception.

Everyone sat down and one of the senior members of the groom's party, a big powerful man with a luxuriant beard and a head-dress consisting of a shock of brown cassowary feathers, delivered a speech, striding up and down in front of his audience and declaiming in a stylized and highly theatrical manner. The bride listened open-mouthed.

The pig-meat had been laid out in a neat rectangle on one side under a casuarina tree, the four brown, smoked heads being laid in a row. When the speech was over another of the visiting men picked up a flank of flesh. The bride's menfolk sat in a line to receive it. As the meat was offered to them by the groom's relative, each man bit off several gobbets of fatty, greasy flesh which he let fall from his mouth into his hand and then laid on a piece of banana leaf. Several wretched dogs observed this distribution of food with pathetic anxiety but none received even the tiniest fragment, for when each man had bitten off his share he took it away to his womenfolk.

The banner was now dismantled, and the feathers and shells laid out in rows on a mat. All the bride's male relations squatted around, and as each item was handed down from the banner there was a long and sometimes heated discussion as to who should ultimately possess it.

When all was finished the visitors took some of the pig-flesh, opened banana leaf packages of cooked vegetables and began to feast. The bride left her family group and sat by her husband's side and for the first time there was an atmosphere of relaxed festivity. One of the men was obligingly seasoning everyone's meal by chewing ginger and spices and spitting on to each piece of meat in turn. It was now evening and as I saw everyone eating with such relish I remembered that I had not had any food myself since early morning. One of the men, seeing me staring, offered me a greasy hunk of pork liberally spattered with chewed ginger. It was a kind and hospitable gesture. Hoping that I might not be considered impolite, I shook my head and pointed to a pile of bananas. Laughingly, the man handed me one and we joined in the wedding breakfast.

CHAPTER THREE
The Animals of Nondugl

FRANK PEMBLE-SMITH is in charge of a very exciting experiment. It was begun just after the war when Sir Edward Hallstrom was told about the huge meadows of kunai grass which surround the Wahgi River by Captain Ned Blood, a soldier who had travelled through the country when he was fighting a guerrilla action against the invading Japanese. Blood argued that although these grasslands were only a few hundred miles from the Equator, they lay at an altitude of over five thousand feet and that therefore they could no more be considered as tropical than much of the prime pasturage of Australia. Furthermore these meadows were empty. No animals grazed them, for New Guinea has no indigenous deer or cattle such as swarm on the plains of Africa. Here surely was an ideal place to raise sheep, and if thriving flocks could be established, the benefits to the local people might be immense.

The Waghi tribes, from force of circumstance, live on a predominantly vegetarian diet. The only animals they have which can provide them with a regular source of meat are the cassowary, a large flightless bird like an ostrich, which is steadily becoming scarcer, and the pig, which is held to be a semi-sacred animal and is so proscribed by ritual and taboo that it is seldom eaten except on ceremonial occasions. Mutton would be an invaluable supplement to their diet.

Further, sociological reports had made it plain that pneumonia and other infections are rampant among the Wahgi peoples. The prevalence of these diseases may be due to the fact that, though it can be bitterly cold in these mountains, the people have no warm clothes. At night they huddle together half-naked in small huts over smoking fires, in an endeavour to keep warm. With wool from the sheep they could make clothes and blankets. If they learned to keep the sheep they might eventually produce more mutton and wool than they needed themselves, sell the surplus, and so be able to buy the products of the outside world which they now lack.

Sir Edward was convinced by Blood's arguments. In 1948 he arranged through the local Government administration to buy from some New Guinea chieftains 340 acres of land on the north side of the Wahgi River. A few months later planes flew in bringing twelve hundred Romney Marsh sheep from Australia. Nondugl was established with Blood as its first manager and the experiment had begun.

From the first it met with considerable problems. The sheep contracted diseases, but this was not a total disaster, for their ailments – sheep worm and fly strike – were not new tropical diseases and could be cured by the same methods as are used in Australia. The main trouble was a more fundamental one. The kunai grass, which looked so lush, turned out to have very little nutritive value. The sheep grazed it willingly, eating huge quantities, yet they grew thinner and thinner. Of the first flock a large proportion died.

Nothing daunted, the men in charge of Nondugl rooted out the worthless kunai and replanted the pastures with grasses from Australia which were known to provide the sheep with first-class food. The labour and money expended was enormous, but even this did not solve the problem, for the imported grasses grew rank and tall in their new environment and the sheep were unable to graze properly. Frank told me all this as he showed me round the station.

Together we walked down to a paddock of rolling ground, newly enclosed with wire fencing. 'This field we've planted with a completely new set of grasses,' he said, 'and so far it looks as though it might be the answer.'

The paddock was full of young lambs and their mothers. To my inexpert eyes they seemed all to be in excellent condition, the ewes being fat and bright-eyed, with thick, firm fleeces, and the youngsters skipping, suckling and wriggling their tails exactly like their relations do back in their original home, the Romney Marshes of Kent.

I glanced away from them and once again I was momentarily shaken by Nondugl's paradoxes, for looking over the shining wire fence stood three half-naked girls with pearl-shell crescents through their noses and a tall bearded man with a shower of golden plumes on his head and a bow in his hand.

'What do they think of it all?' I asked Frank.

'Well,' he replied, 'when we first came here they were very surprised by the sheep but thought that they were merely a sort of freakish variety of pig. Then we brought up cattle and horses and these not only astonished them but actually frightened them. They had never before seen animals so big or imagined that they could exist, for, after all, the biggest animal they had known till then was the cassowary. In time, though, they got used to them and now, of course, most people are quite glad to work on the farm. For one thing, they are anxious to earn some money so that they can buy things from the trade store. Unfortunately, they don't buy the things which you might think they are in most need of – such as blankets for example. Instead they prefer to spend their wages on pearl-shells and paint for their faces!

'I am afraid we have still got a long way to go before we can convince any of them of the value of sheep,' Frank continued. 'We run regular courses here on practical animal husbandry, and people come from all over the territory to attend them. Some of the natives make excellent sheep-men as long as a European is there to watch everything they do, but I'm not certain how many of them either wish to or would be capable of running a small flock for themselves. Many of the local people who work for us only come here for a short time to earn money for one particular purpose — a new wife or something — and then they leave, go back to their village and live in the same way as they have always done.'

Nondugl has now been officially taken over by the Government, but Sir Edward Hallstrom is still closely associated with it. Maybe the sheep experiment will fail. If it does so, it will be a glorious failure. But if it succeeds, the rewards to the native peoples of New Guniea could be great indeed.

The sheep experiment is only one of Nondugl's activities. The other springs from Sir Edward's life-long interest in tropical birds and aviculture. It is the study and conservation of birds of paradise. As a first step, he built huge aviaries in which to assemble a collection of Paradisea which would provide birds for zoos all over the world. But this part of the plan could not be fully implemented, for Australian immigration laws prohibit the entry of any livestock of any kind into Australia for fear of the accidental introduction of disease. This law applies to Paradisea as to everything else, in spite of the fact that each year thousands of birds of many different kinds fly on their migrations from New Guinea to Australia and back again, oblivious of bureaucratic restrictions. The main commercial airlines to eastern New Guinea all run through Australia, so unless a special permit is given — and such exceptions are hardly ever made — any birds from Nondugl must be taken to the outside world by a lengthy sea voyage without calling at any Australian port. This is very hard to arrange, and we ourselves would have to face this problem for we hoped to take back a collection of Paradisea to the London Zoo.

Nonetheless there is now at Nondugl a collection of birds of paradise unparalleled anywhere else in the world, and ornithologists of many nationalities go there to study them.

The man in charge of these birds is Fred Shaw Mayer. He is a thin, greying, gentle person with a slight stoop. If you met him in a city street you might suppose that he was of such a timid disposition that he had never dared to leave his office desk or venture farther abroad than the suburbs of his own town. Yet Fred is one of the greatest of all animal collectors. Born in Australia, he has travelled in some of the

30

wildest and most dangerous parts of the world in search of birds and mammals, insects, and reptiles. He has wandered over both the Dutch and the Australian territories of New Guinea; he has made special journeys to remote islands just to find one particular species of bird. He has caught animals in the Moluccas, in Java and Sumatra and in Borneo, and his collections of specimens are the treasured possessions of many scientific institutions including the British Museum. Many of the creatures he has found on his expeditions have turned out to be previously unknown to science. Three species of birds of paradise were first discovered by him and several creatures bear as part of their scientific name the word 'Shaw-mayeri', a tribute to his skill from the zoologists who named them.

None of this, however, would you suspect when you first meet him. Indeed he is so reticent that it is often difficult to find him at all, for his days are devoted to the birds in his aviaries. He rises well before dawn in order to prepare food for the birds so that they shall be able to feed just after the sun rises as they would do in the wild state. He admits that his native helpers are probably quite capable of mixing the bird food by themselves, but he says mildly that he wouldn't like to risk entrusting it to them in case anything went wrong. At this early hour in the morning it is very cold and Fred habitually wears a number of long woolly cardigans, heavy army boots and an odd deer-stalker hat with flaps which come down over his ears; and in this garb, by the light of a paraffin lamp, he mixes big bowls of special meal with diced paw-paw, pandanus fruit, plantains and boiled eggs. Each group of birds has its own requirements. Some like meat in their diet, so tadpoles and spiders must be found for them; others have a taste for wasp grubs or the yellow of hard-boiled eggs. Sometimes, if other meat is not available, Fred will go to his refrigerator and cut up the fresh mutton which should have provided his own evening meal. The rest of his day is spent walking round the aviaries, tending and cleaning his charges. It is little wonder that he is known by all the local people as Masta Pidgin.

The vast aviaries are heavily planted with trees, bushes and creepers which grow so luxuriantly that it is quite difficult to see the birds for vegetation. This is ideal from the birds' point of view for in these conditions they are living in a state very similar to their own natural environment. It is satisfying, too, for the onlooker, for instead of seeing these splendid creatures

31

in stark white cages on neat cylindrical perches, they are re
vealed to him in exciting glimpses.

There are many different kinds of birds in Fred's care
parrots of all sizes and colours; flocks of huge blue-gre
pigeons each crested with a fan of gauzy feathers spotted wit
silver: and on an ornamental pond, several of one of th
rarest species of duck in the world, Salvadori's Duck, whic
came from a high tarn in the mountains behind Nondugl.

But it was the birds of paradise which almost monopolize
our attention. Here, for the first time, Charles and I saw som
of the birds which hitherto we had known only from illustra
tions in books. Day after day we walked round the aviarie
watching the birds and trying to familiarize ourselves wit
their harsh strident calls so that later, when we went into th
forest, we should be able to identify distant bird-song and s
know what species were in the neighbourhood.

Some of the birds in the aviaries were drab thrush-lik
creatures. These were either hen birds or else young cocks
for the male bird does not grow his magnificent plumes unti
he is four or five years old. When he does, he is so completel
transformed that the linking of hens and immature cocks wit
the fully plumed and quite dissimilar adult males can be ex
ceedingly difficult. Most of Fred's male birds had come t
him as youngsters, for if a Wahgi native caught an adult th
temptation to keep and kill it for the sake of its plumes wa
very often proof against the rewards, high as they were, tha
Fred could offer for it. Many such birds had now been in th
aviaries so long that they had grown their plumes and w
were enthralled by their beauty – the gorgeous Princ
Rudolph's Bird with its haze of sapphire blue plumes rimme
with red; the magnificent, arrogant-looking Princess Steph
anie's Bird, glossy black with a throat patch of rippling gree
iridescence; the bizarre Superb Bird with two curling wire
projecting from its stumpy tail, a green chest, a scarlet back
and a shining yellow cape round its shoulders, a creatur
which failed to match the grace of other species of Paradise
and looked almost as though it were some amateur's first in
expert attempt in designing an extravagantly decorated bird.

I was fascinated by two species in particular. The first wa
one of the smallest, the King of Saxony's Bird of Paradise
This beauty, the size of a starling, is particularly rare and
had never been seen alive outside Australasia. It is the pos
sessor of one of the most remarkable of all feather adorn

32

ments, a pair of long streamers, twice the length of its body, which spring from the back of its head and are decorated with a line of enamel-blue plates, glistening like mother-of-pearl. It is this fantastic creature with its splendidly romantic name which one museum worker is now proposing to rechristen with the mundane, prosaic title of Enamelled False Bird of Paradise.

The second of my obsessions was Count Raggi's Bird of Paradise for this one, which lives in the forests surrounding Nondugl, belongs to the classic and most famous type. It is the local representative of the type which Pigafetti described and which Linnaeus named *Paradisea apoda*. Like Pigafetti's bird it has a green gorget, a yellow head and long filigree plumes sprouting from beneath its wings. It differs in that the original bird had golden plumes whereas Count Raggi's has deep red ones. I watched the Nondugl specimens with the greatest care. They were unfortunately not in full plumage, but they were the kind which Charles and I were hoping to find in the wild so that we might film their courtship dances. They were the creatures which had brought us to New Guinea.

It was only after Fred had finished his all-absorbing day's work in the aviaries that we had any real chance to talk with him. He lives in a small house, with walls and floors made of woven split cane, standing close to the aviaries and surrounded with beds of scarlet cannas. His living-room is furnished simply with a desk, a few chairs, a bare deal table, a refrigerator, and a book-case. On the walls hang a few faded photographs taken on Fred's early expeditions and two original water-colours of birds of paradise which were drawn in the nineteenth century for John Gould's famous treatise on the birds.

It was here that we spent many evenings with him. He sat back in his chair, just beyond the pool of light shed by the pressure lamp standing on the table, fondling Bob, his tame coucal, a large black bird which had a predilection for having its throat tickled. At first he talked little of his own experiences and appeared much more anxious to know what was happening in England. He asked about film stars and about space travel, two topics which perhaps because of their very remoteness seemed to fascinate him, but we managed at last to get him to talk about his early collecting days. He told us how he was usually commissioned to collect animals for wealthy enthusiasts, such as Lord Rothschild, who had such a passion for birds of paradise that he would go down to the docks in London to look through the piles of flattened bird skins, which were imported by milliners, in the hope of finding new species or, equally interesting to him, albino varieties. These he would have mounted and put on exhibition in his private museum at Tring.

But it was the birds of paradise themselves which Fred spoke of with the greatest fervour. Night after night we listened to the quiet, slow words of this gentle and remarkable man as he told us things, gleaned from years of experience which are not yet to be found in any book: the minute differences between two immature birds of the same species which enable you to tell which is a hen and which a cock; the fads and foibles of diet to which one particular species is prone, the knowledge of which might enable a collector to save an ailing bird; the exact valley where an especially rare species could be found. He was very concerned with the problems of protecting the wild birds.

'These people value the plumes so much,' he said, 'that I have to keep all the aviaries carefully padlocked or else they would get in and pluck the feathers from the living birds. Every season, when the plumes are shed, men will come eager to buy them. Only last month one of the King of Saxony birds cast its head-plumes and one of the farm boys offered me three weeks' wages for it.

'They slaughter the birds in enormous numbers and, what is more, the killing now is far greater than it has ever been. When I first came to Nondugl I could hear every evening several species calling in the forest. Now I am lucky if I hear one, and the change is due, I'm afraid, to the spreading of European influence. The authorities, of course, are doing everything they can to protect the birds – it's against the law for a European without a permit to possess a bird of paradise dead or alive – but it is the spread of law and order which is causing the trouble. In the old days a warrior would only dare to hunt for kumuls, as they call them, in the immediate neighbourhood of his hamlet. If he ventured farther out into the forest he ran the risk of being attacked by people from a neighbouring tribe and having his head chopped off. Now when the Government has stopped inter-tribal warfare and everyone is at peace, the young men roam far and wide over the mountains hunting for the birds. It is quite usual for a man, knowing that an important sing-sing is due and that his

ead-dress is a bit dingy, to go off into the forest for a week
nd come back with a dozen dead *kumuls*. As a result the
ead-dresses, these days, are bigger and finer than they have
ver been. And the people now are getting much more par-
cular. If the feathers get soiled and crumpled in a big sing-
ng, they throw them away and go out to hunt for more.

'We did hope,' he added with a sad smile, 'that we might
e able to wean them from paradise plumes by importing dyed
nicken feathers or even peacock feathers, but no – although
ney are interested and amused by such things, they insist that
nly paradise plumes can be used for head-dresses.'

'Is there no chance,' I asked, 'that as the hen birds never
evelop plumes, and even the cocks don't grow them until
ney are several years old, that young cocks and hens will be
ft unmolested to carry on the species?'

Fred shook his head.

'No,' he replied. 'It's perfectly true that unplumed males
o through all the motions of display, but I've never seen a
en pay any attention to them. And that, after all, is just what
ou might expect, for the whole purpose of the plumes is to
tract the hens and stimulate them to mate. Without the
lumes, there is no stimulation.

'The whole situation is getting worse because the local
ibes practise a shifting cultivation, continually felling new
atches of forest for their plantations. They do not replant
ne old ones which, instead of reverting to forest, become
overed by kunai. The Paradisea are essentially forest-living
irds. They cannot exist in kunai areas because they can get
either the cover they like nor the insects and fruit they re-
uire. So when an acre of forest is felled, the means of exist-
nce is automatically denied to a certain number of birds of
aradise.

'That is why,' he continued, 'our aviaries here can be so
aluable. We can use them to show the local boys that their
irds are wonderful creatures worth preserving, not as dead
kins, but as living beings – though that is going to be an up-
ill task. And also by studying the birds in the aviaries, we can
iscover their exact requirements so that if it ever becomes
ecessary to institute reserves we will know exactly what type
f forest and what sort of food supply each species needs.'

We had massive proof of the scale on which the birds are
unted only a few days after Fred had told us all this. Frank
eard that a big sing-sing was to be held at Minj, a place a

35

few miles away across the Wahgi River on the other side of the valley. He drove us over and introduced us to the Assistant District Officer who took us to the sing-sing ground.

It lay about a mile away, a wide expanse of clipped kunai rather like a football pitch, which had been specially cleared for the occasion. Just beyond the ground ran a deep bush filled ravine and beyond rose the southern wall of the valley the Kubor Mountains, steep and yellow-green, clear in the cloudless sky. The ADO told us that the sing-sing dancers were coming down from the mountains to visit a part of their clan which had settled down in the valley. On their way they would stop at each settlement to join with the local people in a dance, so that the whole journey, normally a few hours march, would take several days. He was unsure exactly why they were making the visit. It might be that they were going to transact some business or to make a ritual exchange of food and gifts, thereby reaffirming their tribal bond, or that they were indebted to their clansmen and were going to discharge their obligations by giving a big feast.

'You can never tell,' he said, 'because these jokers will grab the flimsiest excuse for a party,' and with that he left us.

Towards mid-morning a few women from Minj, heavily painted and dressed in full ceremonial costume, appeared on the kunai ground. They had come to see the performance.

After another hour, we heard faint chantings and through binoculars I saw, high up on one of the mountain spurs, a line of tiny figures emerge from a cluster of huts. As I watched Charles spotted another similar group descending one of the ridges away to the right. Every few minutes, the line stopped moving forward and contracted into a blob. As it did so the sound of chanting swelled and was joined by the faint thud of drums. Then the blob elongated into a line again and continued slowly downwards. At last they reached the ravine and disappeared into the bush. The singing grew louder and louder as they climbed unseen towards us until suddenly and dramatically, a dancer crested the near side of the ravine. Clutching his drum, his vast head-dress waving, he moved slowly towards us, chanting as he came. Warrior after warrior followed him in a seemingly never-ending line until by midday, when the sun directly overhead was beating down with almost intolerable brilliance, the sing-sing ground was packed with hundreds of wildly chanting dancers.

They formed themselves in platoons, five in a rank, ten

ranks deep, and, pounding their drums and yelling hoarsely, they stamped fiercely across the ground. Their dance, though simple, absorbed them totally and as the dust thrown up from their naked feet rose around them, caking the rivulets of sweat which ran down their chests and backs, they seemed almost in a state of trance.

Sometimes they halted, but even then they continued to sway to the rhythm of their drums, rising on their toes and bending their knees, the shimmering canopy of their head-dresses undulating like a sea swept by a heavy swell. Many of the men had smeared their muscular bodies with red clay; nearly all of them had thrust leaves of a red shrub in their arm bands and wore bracelets of possum fur. Several were armed with spears or bows and arrows, and one or two carried giant stone axes, the blades fixed in a long, curving piece of wood covered in a decorative basket-work which seemed to serve as a counterbalance to the heavy blade.

Yet above all things, I was overwhelmed by the glory of their head-dresses. Many kinds of paradise birds had been killed to provide these feathers. Nearly every man had two King of Saxony plumes stuck through his nose and fastened in the centre of his forehead so that the feathers formed a superb beaded hoop around the upper part of his face. Some men had so many Saxony plumes that they had included them in their head-dresses as well. One warrior had sixteen of them in addition to the feathers of twenty or thirty Lesser, Count Raggi, Magnificent, Princess Stephanie and Prince Rudolph Birds of Paradise.

It was one of the most spectacular and barbaric sights I have ever seen. I made a rough calculation. There were over five hundred beplumed dancers. Between them, they must have killed at least ten thousand birds of paradise to adorn themselves for this ceremony.

CHAPTER FOUR

Into the Jimi Valley

EVER SINCE I had first read of Nondugl, I had imagined that we should be able to film the display dances of the para-dise birds in the forest close to the station, even though it would doubtless require a great deal of time and patience.

Now, from what Fred had told us, it was clear that we had a much better chance of doing so if we left the Wahgi altogether and went into a wilder and less settled area.

In addition to my plan to film the paradise birds, I had also developed another ambition, for my imagination had been caught by the spectacular stone axes which I had seen being carried by some of the dancers in the Minj sing-sing. Fred told me that when the Wahgi was first discovered, these axes were used throughout the valley but that nowadays the newly introduced metal ones had almost entirely displaced them. Such stone axes as remain were only brought out on ceremonial occasions. No one in the Wahgi still made them but they were traded from tribes living in the Jimi valley over the mountains to the north.

'And what chance is there of finding birds of paradise in the Jimi valley?' I asked.

'Excellent,' Fred replied, 'because there is only a small native population. And not only might you find birds of paradise and an axe factory, but you might also meet some of the pygmies who are supposed to live around there.'

Arranging a trip into the Jimi valley, however, was not easy. In the first place, it was an uncontrolled area and only people with special permits were allowed to enter it. The man responsible for granting permission was the District Commissioner at Mount Hagen Station near the head of the Wahgi valley.

We sent a message to him on the Nondugl radio transmitter asking if we might come to see him, and when the next supply plane landed at Nondugl we climbed on board and flew up to Hagen.

We were shown into the DC's office by one of his ADOs. The Commissioner himself, a bluff Australian in immaculate, neatly pressed khaki, sat behind his desk and looked at us searchingly from beneath heavy eyebrows.

Rather nervously, I explained as best I could what I was proposing: that Charles and I should go into the Jimi valley and spend a month trying to make a film about birds of paradise and the manufacture of stone axes. I added that, if possible, we would like to walk out of the valley along some route other than that we might take on our way in, so that we should see as much as possible of the country.

The DC listened silently until I had finished and then took a map out of a drawer and spread it on his desk.

'Look here,' he said brusquely. 'The Jimi is pretty wild country. So far, we've only sent a few exploratory patrols through it,' and he traced with his finger the dotted lines which crossed a large white blank on his map.

'A couple of years ago pilots who were flying from the Wahgi to Madang on the northern coast reported seeing villages in flames and some of the kanakas came over the hills with stories of women and children being slaughtered wholesale. I sent a patrol in to investigate and they walked into the middle of a tribal war; they were ambushed, several of the policemen were wounded and they had to come out in a hurry. So I went in myself with another patrol officer, Barry Griffin, and a dozen or so armed native policemen. We found a site for a station at a place called Tabibuga and I left Griffin there to build it and to try to restore some sort of order. He's only been out once or twice since and then only for a day or so's rest here at Hagen. Although things seem to be going all right, he's obviously got his hands full. I'm not going to let you go in unless he is quite happy to have you. For one thing, if you start traipsing around the Jimi looking for birds and stone axes you will have to have an escort. He is the only bloke who can provide it and maybe he will reckon he's got other things to do with his policemen than to let them spend their time looking for dicky-birds. Apart from that, he may not want to have you anyway. He's one of those chaps who really like solitude and who ask no more than to be left alone so that they can get on with their jobs. No one has visited him there since he first built the place and he may not like the idea of two strange chaps with no experience of the country arriving out of the blue and dumping themselves on his doorstep. And if he feels that way, I'm certainly not going to order him to have you.'

The DC paused and looked at us hard.

'If he did agree, I would suggest that you go in to Tabibuga by the trail over the mountains along which his supplies are usually carried. It's a two-day march; there's quite a good track now and the kanakas in the villages on the way are, by and large, willing to act as porters. Once you get to Tabibuga, you can sort out with Griffin just how to spend your time. I know he is planning to do a patrol westwards from his station and he might let you go with him. If you want to go out of the valley along a different route, then you'd better cross the Jimi River, go up the other side into the Bismarck Mountains and come out at a place called Aiome in the Ramu valley. There's an airstrip there and no doubt you could charter plane to come and pick you up. Would that suit you?'

'Yes, sir,' I said.

'Very well,' he replied, getting to his feet, 'the next time Griffin comes up on the radio, I'll put the proposition to him. But understand, if he says no, the whole trip is cancelled.'

Suddenly he grinned.

'I hope you blokes like walking,' he added, 'because if you do go in, you have to do a hell of a lot of it.'

Four days later, we received a radio message at Nondugl from the DC: Griffin had agreed to have us, and two of his native policemen would be waiting to escort us in at the Wahgi end of the Tabibuga trail in one week's time.

Immediately we were overwhelmed with the preparations necessary for the journey. We flew back to Lae to get food for ourselves, sacks of rice for the porters, paraffin lamps, saucepans, and tarpaulins to serve as tents. We visited the airline office and arranged that a small, single-engined plane should fly to Aiome on a day just over four weeks ahead to collect us after our journey and fly us back to Nondugl. We purchased bags of salt and beads, knives, combs, mouth-organs, mirrors and pearl-shells with which to pay porters and reward anyone who brought us animals. We also bought plenty of matches and piles of old newspapers, both of which we knew to be highly valued in the remoter parts of the highlands.

We returned to Nondugl and tried to sort out all our gear into 40-lb. loads. This was not easy, for the only scales at Nondugl had just broken and I had to proceed by guesswork. Time after time I filled a patrol box, lifted it and decided that it was so appallingly heavy that it must exceed the stipulated weight as no one could possibly carry it for more than a few minutes. Then I would have to take out some of its contents and replace them with lighter things such as clothes.

On all our previous journeys, Charles and I had only travelled long distances by either truck or boat and in neither case had weight been important. When we had made excursions on foot they had never lasted more than a day or two. As a result, we had never before employed more than three or four carriers. Now, we should be walking for a month and during that time we could not rely on finding either food or shelter. The pile of necessary gear seemed enormous and no matter how carefully I checked my calculations and cut down on personal belongings, I could not avoid the conclusion that we should need at least ten times as many porters as we had ever had before. The prospect appalled me.

One evening I confessed to Fred.

'Maybe we are travelling soft and taking too many luxuries among our food and clothes,' I said, 'but it looks as though we might need perhaps forty porters.'

'Oh! That *is* good,' replied Fred mildly. 'I never seem to be able to manage with less than seventy and you know it can be *so* tiresome trying to recruit as many as that when the natives are not feeling co-operative.'

Nevertheless, I was still quite worried when, on the day before the date of our rendezvous, we found we had so much luggage that we could not possibly pack it all into one jeep. Instead, we had to load the bulk of it on to a farm trailer, hitch it to a tractor and send it ahead driven by one of Frank's senior farm hands. We followed with Frank and the remainder of our gear in the jeep during the afternoon.

Kwiana, the little settlement at the foot of the Tabibuga trail, consisted only of three small huts and a *house-kiap*, a Government rest-house, thatched and built of plaited cane round a timber frame-work. Two huge, muscular native policemen were already there to meet us. Bare-footed and bare-chested, they wore only a neat khaki wrap around their waists and a polished leather belt from which hung a bayonet in its sheath. In appearance they were quite different from the bearded, hook-nosed Wahgi people, for they, like most New Guinea police boys, had been recruited on the coast.

The senior one saluted me smartly.

'Arpi-noon, masta,' he said and handed me a letter. It was from Barry Griffin. He had written that the bearer of the note, Wawawi, was a trustworthy policeman from his staff who knew the trail well and would escort us to Tabibuga. He listed the names of the villages on the route, suggested that we should sleep at one called Karap and ended by saying that he looked forward to meeting us.

While I was reading this, the two police had conscripted some of the villagers and set them to work unloading our gear and stacking it inside the house-kiap.

Wawawi came up and saluted again.

'Key belong box masta,' he said.

As I handed it to him, I experienced exactly the same emotions of apprehension and shame as had once assailed me

41

in the most luxurious and expensive hotel in Hong Kong when the neatly uniformed room-boy had tried to unpack and 'lay-out' my expedition kit. Wawawi's reactions were rather similar to the room-boy's. He undid the padlock of my box, lifted the lid and gazed at the contents with an expression of surprise mixed with horror. In my anxiety to equalize the weight of the boxes. I had felt compelled to include among my own gear some heavier items that a tidier and more methodical man would probably have put elsewhere. Gingerly, Wawawi extracted two tins of jam, a dirty shirt, three paper-backed books, a pair of boots and two pearl-shells wrapped in crumpled newspaper. At last, he found what he wanted, my bed-sail.

This is a long tube of canvas which most people in New Guinea use as a bed when they are travelling in the bush. Having found it, Wawawi called in the other policemen who brought him six long poles. He took two, drove them slant-ingly into the ground about five feet apart, so that they in-clined towards one another forming an inverted V, and lashed the tops together. Then he did the same with two more about seven feet away from the first pair. These were to be the four legs of the bed. The two remaining poles he pushed through the canvas tube, converting it into a sort of stretcher which he placed horizontally so that the stretcher poles rested on the outside of the Vs. Then he sat on it. His weight forced the horizontal poles downwards and the straddle of the bed's legs forced them outwards so that the canvas became taut. Quickly he lashed the side poles in their positions and my bed was ready. After doing the same things with Charles's bed-sail, he and his colleague disappeared.

By now it was getting dark. Charles lit a paraffin lamp and hung it from a beam in the roof, while I produced some *kai-kai* – a tin of meat, and some bananas. As the day faded, I felt chilly and I knew that it would get even colder later on, so before I clambered on to my bed I put on an extra two pairs of khaki trousers, another shirt, and two pullovers. I curled up beneath my blanket and shivered. But it was not only the cold which kept me awake, for as I lay looking unseeingly into the blackness of the roof, the exciting thought swirled round and round in my brain that tomorrow we were going into one of the wildest and least explored territories in the world.

By the time we had finished breakfast the next morning and had repacked our belongings, Wawawi had assembled a large

crowd of villagers in the open space in front of the house-
kiap. They were typical Hagen men, bearded and naked but
for their woven waist-bands and leafy bustles. Most carried in
their belts knives or axes which hung over their bare thighs,
blade to flesh, in what seemed to me to be a most hazardous
position. They appeared to have only recently woken up, for
many were bleary-eyed, their bustles crumpled and soiled. A
few had the smudged remains of painted designs on their faces.
It was still cold for the sun had not yet risen and the men
wrapped their arms around their bare chests to keep warm.

Under Wawawi's direction, our baggage was brought out
and laid in a long line. The porters-to-be stared dejectedly at
the loads, occasionally lifting one to confirm their worst fears
as to its weight and surreptitiously moving away from it towards some other which appeared to be lighter. Wawawi,
however, moved briskly along the baggage, allocating a pair
of men to each item.

When this was complete, Wawawi reclaimed his rifle from
the small urchin who, bursting with importance, had been
holding it for him, looked towards me to see if I was ready
and called an order to the porters. They picked up their loads
and followed Wawawi as he strode up the wide red earth track
which led into the mountains.

For the first mile or so the path ran along the side of a
narrow, steep-walled valley. Beneath us a small river frothed
and sparkled as it tumbled over jams of boulders on its way
to join the Wahgi River. The sun had at last risen, warming
our bodies and dissolving the remnants of mist that hung
around us. One of the carriers yodelled at the top of his
voice 'Hooo–aaah' and prolonged the last lower note as long
as his lungs allowed him. As soon as he started everyone else
joined in, so that the resultant clamour sounded like a continuous long drawn out 'aaaah' with a higher obbligato of
staccato 'hoo's'. It was a noise which was to continue throughout that day and become our constant marching companion
during the next few weeks.

Soon the track steepened and began to zigzag up the spine
of a long grassy ridge. The bare-footed porters plodded
gamely upwards, digging their toes into the steep mud upon
which my nailed boots skidded and slipped. Every hour or so,
Wawawi called a halt, and while the men rested he re-allo-
cated the loads so that each porter took a turn in carrying one
of the heavier boxes.

Towards midday we passed the last of the pleasant casuarina trees and verdant bush that had clothed the slopes so far and entered a thin forest of gaunt trees, their branches trailing withered moss and gnarled creepers. At one point, the track snaked up a series of dripping rock faces which caused the men a lot of trouble. I lingered here to assist where I could, until all the loads had been hauled up it. Just above, the gradient lessened and it seemed that we were approaching the top of the pass. Thin mist was swirling through the bleak forest. I walked slowly, my eyes on the ground, picking my way through boulders and panting slightly, for we were now at an altitude of over eight thousand feet. Ahead, I noticed that the porters had stopped once again. I reflected that it was hardly the best place for a rest and decided to pass them and go over the crest of the col to find somewhere more sheltered. But as I neared them I saw that instead of sitting down the men were clustered round Wawawi and arguing heatedly.

'Dis-fella men, im 'e talk 'e no like go more,' said Wawawi as I neared him.

Certainly they looked cold and tired, but I could see no real reason why they should suddenly go on strike, just when it seemed that the worst part of the climb was over. I did not care to think how we should manage if they did abandon their loads in this remote and lonely spot. In my most persuasive tones I explained that now we were at the top, things would be easier, and from here, I said optimistically, the track will go downhill. Have a good rest, I said, and we will give good rewards when we arrive at the next village; but we must go on. I doubt if they understood what I was trying to say, and it was Wawawi who answered me. The reason they would go no farther, he said, was that the crest of the pass marked their tribal frontier. Beyond that lay the territory of another tribe, who were 'bad-fella too much im 'e kai-kai man.'

'Oh,' said Charles mildly, 'he means cannibals.'

We both laughed, for the situation seemed so like a far-fetched adventure-story as to be farcical. At that moment, I noticed the tip of a feather head-dress projecting from behind a pile of boulders, two hundred yards away in the mist. I blinked in astonishment and then noticed another close by it. My smile faded rapidly.

'Well, cannibals or not,' I replied with slightly forced gaiety, 'I think they are over there waiting for us.'

Suddenly, with ear-splitting yells, a horde of men leaped

44

om behind the rocks and rushed towards us brandishing
nives and axes. My only conscious thought was that I must
rgently convince them that we were friendly. With my heart
anging against my ribs, I walked towards them and extended
y right hand. My meagre vocabulary of pidgin deserted me
nd, rather to my surprise, I heard myself saying loudly, in
hat sounded like absurdly cultured tones, 'Good afternoon'.
his had no effect whatsoever, for they could never have
eard it above their own ferocious yells. Within seconds they
ere upon me. To my total astonishment, several of them
eized my right hand and pumped it up and down. Others
rabbed my left hand and those that could grasp neither
ontented themselves with smacking me violently on the
houlder. 'Arpi-noon, masta, arpi-noon,' they chorused.

Why they should have concealed themselves and then
harged us in such a frightening manner when their intentions
vere in fact friendly puzzled me for a few minutes. Then it
lawned on me that this aggressive display on the frontier was
robably merely a routine ploy in their cold war with the
Vahgi tribes, designed to emphasize their strength and war-
ike character, lest their neighbours should decide that they
vere weak and therefore an easy target for plunder. The
Vahgi men, however, seemed unlikely ever to attack any-
ody as they sat miserably on their heels, shivering in the
lrizzle which was now falling. Wawawi lined them up and
ounted them.

'Four fella ten t'ree, masta,' he said. I unlocked my box,
auled out a bag of coins and handed Wawawi forty-three
hillings for distribution. This was regulation Government
ay for a day's porterage and it was the last time we were
ble to use money before we got back to Nondugl. As soon
s each porter received his pay, he turned and walked away
lown the trail into the mist.

Our new carriers were a more cheerful bunch. They seized
he loads with enthusiasm and, raising a triumphant yell,
noved away at a gallop. The ground began to fall and I
urried on ahead, anxious to get below the clouds and look for
he first time at the Jimi valley. I imagined that it would be
imilar to the Wahgi, a single, wide, grass-filled valley with a
ilver river meandering along the bottom, but when at last I
got a clear view, I saw something very different. Below me
stretched a vast tract of wild country, a complex maze of
nterlocking ridges and mountains, entirely covered with

forest. I could see no rivers, no stretches of kunai grass and no villages; nothing but an endless rucked carpet of trees.

The ridge we were descending seemed to run towards a small valley, close at hand on our left. One of the tribesmen came and stood by my side. I pointed to the valley. 'Jimi?' I asked. The man burst into a roar of laughter, shook his head and pointed into the far distance, screwing up his eyes. Then with the patient air of a teacher explaining some rudimentary fact to a particularly stupid child, he held his left hand in front of my face and, one by one, touched four of his out stretched fingers.

'Good heavens,' I said to Charles, 'we've got to cross another four valleys before we get to the Jimi.'

'More likely he means we've got another four days' walking,' Charles replied dourly.

I tried to find out exactly what my companion was attempting to indicate with his four fingers, but without success. Indeed, I never did discover. It was merely one of the occasions on which our lack of a common language seemed an insuperable barrier. I was overwhelmed with a surge of loneliness which was not dispelled even when the chanting swarm of porters caught up with us. We were entering a new primeval land in which we had no real place. It was true that ahead of us, in a fold of one of the mountains, among the infinity of trees, one Australian had made a clearing in the forest and built himself a house, but he had created no more than a minute pockmark on the landscape. The track at my feet was his creation also, but it was only a slender thread linking us to him. If I left it and walked for five minutes in some other direction, I should be on ground which no European had ever seen before.

We followed the path trustingly as it wound along the crest of ridges, zigzagged down steep muddy slopes and dived into the forest. Every mile or so, we met groups of tribesmen who were standing on the path waiting, no doubt, to see what the shouting was about. As we passed, they enthusiastically attached themselves to our caravan and added their voices to the clamour.

Towards three o'clock, we reached the first sign of habitation which we had seen since we had left the Wahgi, a low palisade of sharp stakes broken only by a narrow gap, flanked by posts painted with tribal markings. Half an hour later we stepped from the forest into a village – two lines of thatched huts strung along the crest of the ridge, enclosing a bare expanse of red earth and girdled by a ring of casuarina trees. The entire population had assembled to meet us, the women sitting in one group, the men in another. The luluai and his lieutenants stood at the far end in front of the largest hut, which I guessed to be the house-kiap. As we threaded our way towards him, through the squatting villagers, they raised a deafening yell of welcome. The luluai escorted us into the house-kiap and our first day's march was over.

Wawawi once again supervised the stacking of the baggage and paid off the porters, this time in tablespoonfuls of salt. Each man received it in a piece of leaf, wrapped it up carefully, tucked it in his belt and wandered out of the village back to the forest. While our beds were being erected I sat outside on the edge of the ridge, resting my back against a casuarina, and scanning the trees in the valley below me. To my delight, I heard the call of a Lesser Bird of Paradise, but though I searched with my glasses for a long time, I could not see the bird itself. As evening fell, clouds rolled up from the valleys below until the village alone remained clear. Charles and I made our supper and stiffly went to bed.

We were woken, just after dawn, by a vociferous yodelling. The luluai was standing among the casuarinas, his hands cupped round his mouth, his voice echoing over the cloud-filled valleys. In response to his calls, forty or fifty porters assembled in front of the house-kiap; many of them I recognized as the men we had met on the road during the previous afternoon. Just before we moved off, it began to rain. It was cold and uncomfortable, but our boxes were watertight and the carriers merely pinned a few broad leaves in their skull caps to keep their heads dry. By midday, we had passed through the cloud layer and the rain stopped.

Our progress now became a triumph, for as we went we collected, like a snowball, more and more tribesmen who trotted along with us. The spasmodic hooo-aaah's of the previous day now became continuous. I yearned for a little peace and quickened my pace to outdistance the carriers, but the main supporting party of chanting men ran after me and it was impossible to escape.

At one o'clock we had a sudden distant view through a small gap in the bush and I saw below us a tiny red spot in the dark green forest. Through my binoculars I could distinguish a few rectangular buildings and in the middle, a flag flying from the top of a mast. It was Tabibuga.

An hour later we reached it. Our entry was dramatic in the extreme. Our escort now numbered several hundred. Our vanguard consisted of thirty or forty warriors with painted faces and feather head-dresses who advanced in short spurts. At the end of each run, they redoubled their shouts, stamped furiously with their right feet and waved their knives and spears. Wawawi had reclaimed his rifle, which for most of the day had been carried by one of the local men, and was marching just behind us with it on his shoulder in the correct military manner. Our porters, shouting with excitement, were doing their best in spite of their loads to run and caper like the unencumbered warriors ahead. As we flooded on to the huge parade ground of Tabibuga, I saw that we were awaited by at least a thousand people. They added their screams to the general bedlam and cleared out of the way as our advance guard cantered forward towards the large building which dominated the station. On the veranda I could see a man in white sitting reading, totally unperturbed by the riotous demonstration all around him. He did not even look up. When we were no more than twenty yards away from him, he raised his head, got to his feet and slowly walked towards me.

'Griffin,' he said, as he shook my hand. 'Sorry about all the noise. My chaps are bit excited because you are the first Europeans who've come in since I've been here. Guess they thought I was the only one in existence and they're probably pretty shattered to find that there are a couple more.'

CHAPTER FIVE

Tabibuga

TABIBUGA WAS Barry Griffin's own creation. His first task on arriving in the valley had been to pacify the warring tribes and he decided therefore to establish his patrol post in the middle of the most troubled area, which lay not in the flat lands of the lower Jimi but high among the mountains and gullies near the head of the valley, many miles from the river itself. To create a suitably level site in this rugged country, he had cut a wide platform a hundred yards across in the side of a ridge. This now forms the parade ground. Along one side of it are ranged Barry's office, the court-room from which he administers justice, and a trade-store stocked with knives and axes, cloth, beads, paint, and shells. Below it lie the quarters of his native staff, vegetable gardens, pens for pigs and goats, and a *house-sick* – a tiny hospital administered by two native medical orderlies. On the crest of the ridge, beneath a tall pine and overlooking the station, stands his own house, built so close to the ridge's edge that the wash-room overhangs it and is supported by stilts, a convenient arrangement for the water from the canvas bucket which serves as a shower can fall straight through the loosely woven cane floor and drain away down the hillside.

Apart from the bathroom, his house consists only of one large room with glassless windows closed by shutters, and a cook-house connected to the main building by a short covered passage. Everything inside was immaculately arranged. Magazines were stacked in neat piles according to their date, their type, and whether they were read or unread. The boots by the door stood in an orderly line. The blankets on the camp-bed in the corner were carefully folded and covered with an embroidered counterpane. The table was bare except for a bowl of forest flowers. Nowhere was there the litter of domestic trivia which most people accumulate. It was the home of a man with a passion for tidiness.

Barry himself was tall and slim with closely cropped black hair. As we sat talking politely in his house, I could detect no expression on his face which would help me decide whether he was glad or annoyed at our arrival. He spoke softly with the minimum movement of his lips. With a curt order he called his house-boy, who entered carrying three bottles of beer on a tray. They had been brewed in Australia and here in the Jimi they were as valuable as bottles of the best champagne in London. As we drank he seemed to relax.

'Well,' he said, 'I'm both surprised and relieved to meet you. All I knew from Hagen radio was that you were film makers and ornithologists, which seemed to me an odd mixture, and I didn't know whether to expect Hollywood types in loud clothes and horn-rimmed spectacles or elderly bearded blokes with butterfly nets. It's good to discover that you are neither. Anyway, come and eat.'

Apart from the bread and potatoes the meal had been produced entirely from tins – lambs' tongues, asparagus tips and fruit salad – although Barry made deprecating remarks about

49

it, clearly he had broached a carefully hoarded store of luxuries to provide it. I was anxious not to presume too much on his hospitality and suggested that we should pitch camp farther along the ridge and sleep there on our bed-sails. Barry quietly replied that he had arranged for us to sleep in the house, should we wish to do so, and as night fell the house-boy came in again and set up two more camp-beds complete with blankets.

I awoke before dawn. Through the half-open shutters drifted a babel of bird song. Hurriedly I dressed and, leaving the other two sleeping, I grabbed my binoculars and crept out of the house. A few yards outside the door, and on the opposite side to the parade ground, the ridge fell towards a forest-filled valley which was echoing with strident bird-calls. I sat against the solitary pine, sweeping the trees below me with my glasses. I had been there for over an hour before the house-cook announced his presence beside me with a tactful cough and told me that breakfast was ready.

Barry was silent over breakfast, but I was so excited by what I had seen that I became extremely talkative.

'I can't tell you how thrilled I am to be here,' I said to him. 'Already I've seen five fully plumed Lesser Birds of Paradise flying in the forest just below us. There must be thousands of ornithologists who would give anything to stay in this house even for only a few days. How wonderful it must be to live here throughout the year with these gorgeous creatures on your very doorstep.'

I continued to enthuse but could get no reaction from him.

'It's just possible,' Charles murmured, 'that Barry doesn't particularly *like* birds of paradise.'

Barry looked up from his plate of porridge.

'That's not true,' he said, seriously. 'I love them. Nicely browned and with a good gravy they're delicious.'

He grinned.

'Actually,' he added, 'I've never tasted birds of paradise but the only way I really appreciate any of your feathered friends is on the dining table. I'm afraid I'm going to be a disappointment to you chaps, because somehow I can't get excited about the birds and the bees. I tried to once. An American wrote to me offering lunatic prices for some of the butterflies that are supposed to live around here. It seemed to me quite a good way to make a little extra money, so I had killing bottles, setting boards and all the rest of the paraphernalia sent in, but when it came to it I felt so foolish stumbling about the forest with a butterfly net, I gave it up.

'The thing I can't stand, though, is tame birds cluttering up the place. Some of my cops once started to keep cockatoos but the noise and the mess the brutes created was so disgusting that I made a station regulation prohibiting the keeping of pets.'

Charles and I looked at one another glumly.

'That's why the local lads looked so astonished the other day,' Barry continued, 'when I told them that the next time they came in to the station, I wanted them to bring in all the wild birds and beasts they could find. They thought that their kiap had gone raving mad until I explained that when you two chaps came in the station regulations would be temporarily lifted.

'Mind you, I doubt if they will bring any birds of paradise or any information about the dancing trees. They are pretty possessive and secretive about their birds. If a man has a dancing tree on his land, all the birds that come to it are reckoned to be his property even though they fly over other people's ground. He may watch a young bird for several years waiting for it to grow its plumes, so he gets rather upset if, just when its feathers are at their best, someone else manages to shoot it before he does. Of all the cases which I have to try in the native court, the ones which cause the most trouble and bloodshed are quarrels over land, women and birds of paradise – and not necessarily in that order. So you can understand that they don't like strangers knowing where the trees are. However, I've asked the station luluai to come up this morning and I'll see if I can get him to tell you anything.'

When the luluai arrived, he stood at the door, nodding respectfully as Barry spoke to him in rapid pidgin.

'If you go along with him,' Barry said to me, 'he will show you a dancing tree.'

I followed the luluai down from the house, across the parade ground, through the little village that lay beyond, and along the steeply descending muddy track. Soon we had left the station buildings far behind and were walking through dense forest, a moist tangle of trees and creepers interspersed with beautiful tree ferns. At last we came to a giant fig tree which soared high above the bush surrounding it. A ladder of notches had been cut in its massive runnelled trunk. They must have been made a long time previously, for their edges

51

were softened and concealed by over-growing bark. Looking up into the branches, I could see, forty feet above the ground, a crude wooden cabin. The luluai explained by a mixture of dumb show and pidgin that the birds came to dance on a bough a few yards away from the cabin. When the time was ripe he would climb into the hide during the night and wait until dawn with his bow and arrows ready. As the sun came up, the cock bird of paradise would come to the branch and begin his performance. Then, a single twang of the bow string would turn a strutting, vibrant fountain of plumes into a limp, bloody corpse.

With difficulty, I climbed up the trunk, using dangling sinewy creepers as hand-holds, until I could see the bough on which the birds danced. It had been used recently for its bark bore fresh scratches and was shorn of twigs. Remembering the age of the notches below, it was clear that the hide had been in use for many years. Generations of birds must have been slaughtered here.

The foliage of the fig tree was so luxuriant that it was not possible to get a clear view of the place where the bird danced either from the ground or, as I now discovered, from the hide itself. I could see only enough to give me a sight for a shot with a gun – but not with a camera. We should not be able to film here, even if any birds still survived to dance.

When I descended I asked the luluai if plumed birds still came to the tree. He shook his head. As we walked back to the station we passed his own hut. He left me for a moment, crawled into the hut and emerged holding a dried bird of paradise skin, with a splinter of bamboo thrust through its beak so that it could be fixed in a head-dress, its gorgeous plumes uppermost. He had shot it a week earlier in the fig tree.

*　　　　*　　　　*

The next day, the parade ground was invaded by a thousand Milma tribesmen. They came not from the country close to Tabibuga but from an area almost a day's march away on the other side of one of the bigger tributaries of the Jimi River. Two years ago they had been fighting with the Marakas, the local Tabibuga people, and it was this war that had made the establishment of the patrol post an urgent necessity. When Barry arrived he found that the Milmas had been driven from their farms and villages by the Marakas and

52

one of his first actions had been to order the Marakas to relinquish their newly acquired territory and to reinstate the Milmas on their original tribal lands. Now they came to the patrol post once a week bringing loads of cassava, paw-paws, yams, and sugar-cane which Barry required to feed his station staff, and which he exchanged for knives, shells, and cloth from his store. Barry had been compelled to allot a special day of the week for these visits, so that he could ensure that there were no large parties of Marakas on the station in case the meeting of the two enemies might cause old quarrels to flare up again.

The Milmas at first sight resembled the Wahgi people for they were bearded, their faces were painted, they had pierced their noses to carry pearl-shell crescents, and they were dressed in broad waist-bands with crotcheted laps in front and bustles of leaves at the back. Yet they had about them a wilder, more savage air. Nearly all wore the brown, furry tailskin of a tree kangaroo slung from their necks and hanging down their chests. Their head-dresses were not made up exclusively of paradise plumes but contained feathers from owls, eagles, and cockatoos, and these, though they were faded and bedraggled, invested the men with an air of barbaric virility which contrasted markedly with the gaudy but faintly effete opulence of the Wahgi men. And nearly all of the Milmas were armed with knives, bows and arrows, huge three-pronged spears and war-lances ten feet long.

These were the people that Barry had asked to bring us animals and birds, and after he had introduced us in a short speech which was relayed to them by the station interpreter, or *turnim-talk*, they came up to us, one by one, and presented us with enigmatic bundles.

As we unpacked each one and examined its contents, I assessed its value in terms of rarity and condition, and Barry priced it accordingly in terms of trade goods. The first was an oval parcel wrapped in leaves and carried in a neatly tied harness of creepers. I opened it and found the gigantic green egg of a cassowary. Although we did not want it, we paid the man a handful of blue beads for it. The second man, with an air of unconcealed pride, held out a splinter of bamboo on which were spitted the corpses of several dozen identical beetles. In spite of the fact that he had slightly misunderstood Barry's request, he had obviously spent a great deal of time collecting the creatures and we paid him two handfuls of beads. The third and fourth offerings were also eggs, those of a brush-turkey, white and, though smaller than the cassowary, still very large. The fifth man handed me a length of bamboo stopped at its open end with a twist of grass. I unplugged it and carefully shook out on to the ground a snake. The turnim-talk leaped backwards with an unintelligible but vehement expostulation. I took a stick, pinned the reptile's head to the ground and, seizing it with my thumb and forefinger at the back of its neck, picked it up. It was a beautiful emerald green python, decorated with a broken line of white scales along its spine. I knew the London Zoo would wish to have such a handsome and interesting snake but, to my sorrow, I saw that it had a bad wound on its mouth from which it would soon die.

Next came three quite different objects. They were all made of stone – a slim polished axe-head with the smooth tactile beauty of a Chinese jade, a mace-head of rough pitted stone shaped like a pierced pineapple and the size of a tennis ball, and a heavy stone bowl. This last object belonged to a type which, although well known, is nevertheless an enigma. The tribesmen in the central highlands frequently come across such bowls when they are digging in their fields. But they themselves have never made them, nor are they sure what their use was. It seems likely that they are the relics of an earlier people who lived in the New Guinea mountains before the present population arrived. Sometimes the bowls are found together with stone pestles and for this reason they are termed mortars. Yet no one knows what was ground in them. They are too small to be used for preparing vegetables. It has been suggested that they may have been used to make paint pigments; but no traces of any such substances has ever been detected in them.

The one I held was an unornamented but perfect example. I asked the man who gave it to me what he used this mysterious object for. He explained that he filled it with water and used it as a mirror. Later, I tried this and certainly it served this purpose very well, the heavy stone keeping the water remarkably free of ripples. Nevertheless, the discovery of pestles with other examples meant that this could scarcely have been its original function.

The last offering was even more exciting. A warrior stretched out his brown hand and I saw, cowering in his palm, two tiny fledglings. Their bodies were covered with quills, just poking through the goose-pimpled skin, which gave them the bluish tinge of an unshaven chin. They had disproportionally large beaks of a shape which was unmistakably that of a parrot, but until they were fully fledged I could not be certain as to exactly what they were. I hoped that they might be Dwarf Fig Parrots, a particularly rare and interesting branch of the parrot family which occurs only in New Guinea.

It was imperative to give them some food immediately and I took them back to the house, so beginning a process which over the next few days was to transform Barry's immaculate home into something resembling the annexe of a zoo. He viewed the parrot's arrival with stoical calm. Fortunately, the little creatures were old enough to be able to eat by themselves and readily nibbled bananas. But bananas alone would not, I knew, sustain them for long and it was vital that I should persuade them to eat some seeds as well. I had brought with me a small supply of sunflower seeds but the parrots, never having seen such things before, did not regard these shiny, polished, tasteless objects as food. Accordingly I spent a long time that day – and many days that followed – cracking each seed, extracting the kernels and sticking them into bananas. The chicks in their eagerness to eat their bananas inadvertently took some of the kernels and soon acquired a taste for them. Eventually, before we left New Guinea, the little birds were shelling the seeds for themselves and eating them with enthusiasm. By this time, too, they had fledged completely and developed brilliant green bodies, scarlet foreheads and cheeks and a small patch of blue above their eyes, showing that they were, indeed, Dwarf Fig Parrots. No bigger than sparrows, they were the most captivatingly tame of all the creatures we finally took back to the London Zoo and the first of their kind ever to be seen there.

*   *   *

Two days later, the Marakas came into the station. They too had come to trade, but this particular day was for them an especially important one. Barry had arranged by radio with the DC in Hagen for a consignment of supplies to be dropped to him by air. It was not that he needed the goods in a hurry, nor that he could not have arranged their transport by carrier-line over the mountains, which would have been a very much cheaper method. His purpose was rather to use the air-drop as a piece of propaganda to emphasize to the local people that he was not merely a lone individual but could call on support in particularly miraculous form from a world outside the Jimi The Marakas, however, were indifferent when he told them that a *balus*, the pidgin word for aeroplane, would come over and drop cargo, and when he asked one of the farmers to lease a suitable flat stretch of land below the station so that it might be cleared to serve as a dropping zone, the tribesman had refused. The only land Barry could secure was a small steep kunai slope several miles away from the station itself, which hidden as it was among the mountain spurs, was very unsuitable for the purpose.

Several hundred Marakas followed us and the station policemen as we went down to the site in the morning. The police set them to work, clearing the few bushes that remained on the slope and lighting fires of green wood and grass at the four corners to provide smoke signals. In the centre of the zone, they laid out a triangle of white cloth as a further means of identification.

Prompt on time, an aircraft appeared over the mountains It circled above us at a considerable height, assessing the best line of approach. Then it disappeared behind one of the mountains. There was silence except for the uninterested chatter of the Marakas. They were not impressed by what they had seen so far; after all, baluses were continually flying over their country at such heights. They were merely small silver birds that made a faint drone.

Suddenly, with a deafening roar, the plane skimmed over the ridge behind us, so low that we could recognize the pilot As it passed us, a dozen sacks were pushed out of the open door in the fuselage. They landed accurately in the centre of the dropping zone, bouncing high in the air. The plane thundered on, climbed steeply, banked to avoid the mountain ahead of it and disappeared again behind the skyline.

The Marakas shrieked and jumped with excitement. They yodelled, they pointed in amazement to the place on the horizon where the plane had vanished and shook one another enthusiastically. Never before had they seen a plane so low so loud or so huge, and never before had one disgorged bags of cargo. Several men began to run on to the slope to retrieve the bags and the police boys only managed to get them back to safety a few minutes before the plane reappeared and dropped another load.

After the fourth run, it rolled its wings in farewell, climbed high and droned away south until it was lost in the clouds.

Barry gave the order for the bags to be collected and the Marakas, in a yelling horde, swept over the kunai. The plane had dropped sixty sacks of rice, salt and flour, and one containing a leg of fresh mutton and some mail. Each had been double-bagged and, although all the inner sacks had burst on the first impact, in only one case had the outer one split and any of the contents been lost.

We returned to Tabibuga, leaving the police to supervise the transport of the cargo. We waited in Barry's office. Soon the Marakas arrived, chanting and dancing exultantly, carrying the sacks on poles. They set the loads down in front of the office and danced round them in celebration. One of the headmen then began a long, shouted oration, marching up and down, trailing his lance and waving an axe. After another five minutes, another man took his place and delivered another speech.

Barry translated for us.

'The Wahgi men who came over the hills to trade kumul feathers call us bush kanakas and beasts of burden. They say we are no good because we have to carry cargo into our valley on our backs while theirs comes in a balus from the sky. But now the balus has come to us too. Now we have salt and knives and beads from the sky. Now we are the same as the Wahgi men.

'For this, we have to thank our kiap. He is the man who stopped our wars which made us so unhappy before he came. He is the man who settles our quarrels with justice. He is the man who brings us metal knives and axes, and now he is the man who has called the balus down from the sky. Let us thank our kiap.'

Barry listened impassively as man after man made his speech. At length the declamations were over. Barry turned to go into his office.

'Flannel,' he said. 'Let's hope they remember all that when I try to get some decent ground for the next air-drop.'

CHAPTER SIX

The Axe-makers

THE RIDGE on which Barry had built his house proved to be an excellent vantage point for watching birds. Every day we saw several Paradisea but always they were so far distant that even with our most powerful telephoto lens we were unable to film them adequately. We also occasionally caught glimpses of them when we walked in the forest but our views of the birds were so fleeting that again photography was impossible. To film them, we had to find some place to which they paid regular visits and then to build a hide close to it so that we could wait, with our cameras ready, for the bird to appear. A dancing tree or a nest would provide just such a situation, but though we searched we were unable to discover either, and the local people, as we expected, professed complete ignorance.

In the course of our explorations, we found several snakes, a stick insect nearly a foot long, a number of brilliantly coloured tree-frogs, a swarm of huge caterpillars, and many other small creatures which provided subjects for our cameras but these animals seemed to us to be very inadequate substitutes for our main quarry – the birds of paradise.

In the chilly evenings, we sat with Barry around the stove heaped with blazing wood that stood by one wall of his living-room. He seemed reluctant to talk about his job or the people in his charge, preferring, after his day's work on the station was finished, to dismiss from his mind everything Papuan and to return to as European an atmosphere as possible. It was an understandable attitude. To live alone in this wild, isolated area and to become too intimately embroiled in the traditions and social life of the surrounding primitive people might well endanger a man's own standards and beliefs, unless he possessed profound and unshakeable religious convictions. Barry was not a deeply religious man and he safeguarded himself by retiring each evening into a cocoon of Western customs which he had spun with the aid of his magazines and books, his radio and his own strict observance of domestic etiquette. My own initial reaction on entering a wild area is to discard precisely these things in the knowledge that within a few months I shall be back among them. Nonetheless, we too found it very

pleasant warming ourselves in front of the fire, reading novel-
ettes, with the sound of music relayed from Australia, America
or Britain, crackling and fading on the wireless.

It was on these evenings that we planned our route to
Aiome. Barry had never made the complete journey in one
trek but had travelled along most of the route at one time or
another on his patrols, and with the aid of his own sketch
maps we were able to draw up a time-table. He told us that
stone axes were still made at a village called Menjim which
lay two days' march down the Jimi valley, on the same side
of the river and about as far from it as Tabibuga. The journey
to Menjim would not be an easy one for the only existing
track crossed numerous tributary valleys running down at
right-angles to the Jimi River, and to travel from one to the
other would involve each time toiling up steep jungle-covered
slopes to a high pass and then descending several thousand
feet to the next river. Menjim lay on one of these tributary
rivers, the Ganz. From there we planned to walk down the
Ganz valley in one day to the Jimi itself, where, at a place
called Tumbungi, we could cross it by a native-made cane
suspension bridge. On the other side lay the Bismarck Mountains, the country of the pygmies. To cross the main range
we should have to climb to over six thousand feet, and it
would take us five days of hard marching to complete our
journey down to Aiome, in the valley of the Ramu, the
huge river which drains the northern flanks of the Central
Highlands of New Guinea and empties into the Bismarck
Sea.

As a result of these calculations, we knew it would take
at least eight full days of travel to reach Aiome. The date for
our rendezvous there with the charter plane was unchangeable
and if we spent too long at Tabibuga, we might be unable to
spare any time for filming on the journey ahead. I became
anxious to leave. Barry, however, was unexpectedly faced with
some local problems on the station which he felt he could not
abandon until they had been settled, so we agreed that Charles
and I should go on ahead to Menjim, and that he should join
us there as soon as he could.

We left early one morning, six days after we had arrived
at Tabibuga. Once again Wawawi came with us. He himself
led the way, Charles and I followed, and behind us came a
long, winding column of porters, three of the more responsible and careful ones carrying the cages containing the two

little parrots and some snakes. For the first hour or so the journey was deceptively easy, the track descending gently down kunai ridges and occasionally passing through small patches of forest. Wawawi sent runners ahead to conscript relays of porters and as we reached each new tribal territory we found men waiting on the frontier to carry our baggage onwards.

At about ten o'clock we reached Kwibun, the first village on the route. Here we stopped for a rest. The local people collected in a group around us chattering with excitement, and while the porters refreshed themselves with snacks of cold cassava, I unlocked the patrol box which contained our trade goods and extracted a large pearl-shell. We had come to look for 'stone-axe' and 'all-kind pidgin' which 'no got wound', I explained, waving the shell in the air, and I would exchange 'dis-fella keena' for a good example of either. The villagers listened to me wonderingly. Then one of them left the group, went into his hut and returned with an axe.

Like the ones we had seen at the Minj sing-sing, it was T-shaped, the stone blade having a long, curving, wooden counterbalance, but it was smaller and completely covered with a black, sticky tar. Clearly it had been lying disused for many years above the smoking fire in the rafters of the tribesman's hut, and he had only brought it to me because, of all his implements, it was the one he least valued. It was, however, exactly what I wanted, for its obvious signs of age implied that it had been made, and probably used in battle, before the arrival of any metal tools into the Jimi, and I gladly traded it for the pearl-shell.

No one produced anything else of interest, so we left and continued westwards. After another two hours' marching, the spring began to disappear from my stride. I had assumed that in this rainy country there would be many streams and consequently I had not brought water-bottles. But the sun shone fiercely from a clear sky, scorching my skin, the dust from the kunai grass caked my lips and my throat became agonizingly parched. We marched on for mile after mile without finding the smallest rivulet which could provide us with a drink. Charles seemed to feel the lack of water even worse than I. He was sweating so profusely that not only was his shirt soaked but his trousers back and front became saturated and frequently he was able to wring a cupful of liquid from the hems at the bottom of his trouser-legs. This was very worrying for although the day was hot, the journey was no more strenuous than the one we had made to Tabibuga when Charles had not perspired in this abnormal way, and I feared that he might be suffering from a fever of some sort. With no drink to make good this constant drain of water from his body, he soon began to feel really ill, but in spite of this he gamely trudged on.

Early in the afternoon, we descended into a deep valley and found at the bottom a wide river at which Charles at last was able to slake his thirst. We took a protracted rest, and then began the long climb up steep forest-covered slopes on the other side. Barry had recommended that we should sleep that night at a village called Wum, and at last I thought I could see it in the distance on the crest of a high knoll. It looked impossibly far away and the two hours it took us to reach it seemed interminable. Wawawi strode at my side, laughing at my weariness, and we entered the village together. I sat outside the small house-kiap, which Barry had ordered to be built on his last visit, and called for water. The village luluai brought it to me in long hollow stems of bamboo. I drank greedily. I sluiced the cool water over my chest. I poured it wastefully over my face and neck and washed away the dust. 'This place Wum, im number one place true,' I said to Wawawi. 'Walkabout finis. Me like die now.'

'Name belong dis place, Tsenga,' said Wawawi cheerfully. 'Wum long-way more.'

'Wawawi,' I said with decision, 'me sleep 'long dis place. Makim bed, quick time.'

When Charles hobbled into the village an hour later, I had a large mug of tea waiting for him and his bed ready. He collapsed exhausted on to it and confessed that he had nearly been sick on the way up.

The next day he felt considerably better, but the journey was if anything harder than the previous day's. Several times we had to descend a thousand feet, slithering and skidding down a muddy forest track, ford a river and then panting and sweating, trudge up the mountain on the other side of the valley to regain our original height. Each time, I hoped that Wawawi would tell me that the river in the valley over the next divide was the Ganz, but it was not until the late afternoon as we sat resting on the crest of a pass that he announced that Menjim lay immediately below us. By this time I had gained my second wind and I took the steeply winding path at a run. The Menjim villagers having heard the chants of our carriers had come part way up the track to meet us, and as I trotted past them, unwilling to break the rhythm of my pace, they cheered and grinned and momentarily clasped my hands so that I felt as though I were an Olympic athlete entering the stadium for the last lap of the marathon.

The Ganz valley was beautiful and, as it was the end of this stage of our journey, it seemed to me to be particularly so. The river frothed and cascaded through a forest of giant pine trees, and on its banks in a spacious clearing stood Menjim itself. The house-kiap was large and roomy and as the porters carried in our loads, the villagers brought us gifts of pineapples, paw-paws and bread-fruit. Only one of them, a young man with a large leaf and two tufts of cockatoo feathers stuck in his woolly hair, understood any of my pidgin. Proud of his unique ability, he seated himself on the veranda and waited patiently to act as turnim-talk whenever we might require him.

It was he who agreed the next morning to take us to the place where the axes were made. It lay only a few minutes from the village on the hillside lower down the valley. A group of men were sitting around a fire by the side of a small stream, chipping pieces of stone and gossiping and singing as they worked. As we arrived they got to their feet and clustered round us while Turnim-talk explained to them in a patronizing way who we were and what we had come to see. I asked where the stone came from and, in explanation, one of the older axe-makers waded into the stream. After a few minutes' search, he bent, heaved up a large dripping boulder, and staggered back to lay it at our feet. It was roughly oblong in shape and several of the axe-makers squatted beside it and began to talk volubly. One of them scratched lines along its length with a pebble, gestured to a point on it, and explained that if it were struck there it would split lengthways.

'Lookim,' said Turnim-talk admiringly, 'dis good-fella stone too much. Im workim big-fella axe.'

Certainly an axe blade the length of the boulder would be gigantic, and much larger than any we had seen so far.

The suggested method of cleavage was not, however, accepted by everybody and several more men made alternative recommendations. The old man listened patiently to them all. Then, his mind made up, he picked up a heavy stone, placed it carefully on the point on which he proposed to hit the boulder and lifted it above his head. He stood poised, then hurled the stone down with all his strength.

There was a moment's silence, then a shout of laughter from all the axe-makers. The boulder had split, but across its length, exactly at right-angles to the direction which had been so carefully planned. Everyone seemed to regard this misfortune as a great joke.

Turnim-talk wiped tears of laughter from his eyes.

'Two-fella lik-lik akis, t'a's-all,' he said.

When the old man had recovered from the humour of the situation, he lifted his stone maul again and attacked the bigger of the two halves. This time he had more success, for it cleaved neatly into long smooth flakes. He continued smashing the remnants of the boulder until it was reduced to a vast quantity of chips and over a dozen flakes. He selected the largest of them and surrendered the rest to the other men. Then he sat down, took a pebble and patiently began chipping his chosen fragment into the approximate shape of an axe head. Every few minutes he picked up the axe blade-to-be and, holding the narrower end lightly between his thumb and fore-finger, tapped the lower end with his pebble so that the stone rang. Each time he did so he smiled broadly and I assumed he was able to tell from the tapping sound whether or not the stone was perfect and uncracked.

'Finis im a kis long dis place?' I asked Turnim-talk.

'No got,' he replied. 'Come.'

We followed him down the stream to the main river and there we found an even larger group of men sitting among the jumble of boulders at the river's edge, grinding and polishing their axe blades. They were using whetstones of a coarse sandstone which Turnim-talk informed us also occurred as boulders in the river. There was no uniformly accepted method of working. One man had embedded his whetstone in the soft stem of a banana palm and, with this in front of him, was rhythmically rubbing his axe blade back and forth on it, stopping every few minutes to dip the blade in the river swirling by him and examine its progress. Another worked in the opposite way: he had laid his blade on the ground and was filing it methodically with a rather smaller whetstone. Some, who had finished the main work on the axe head, were carefully bevelling the curved cutting edge. Others were shaping the wooden counter-weights, weaving the decorative cane covering and binding on the wooden hafts.

I asked Turnim-talk how long it took to complete one axe.

'Some-fella time, t'ree fella moon,' he replied. 'Some-fella time, six-fella moon.'

If this were so, it was only because the men approached their work in such an unhurried spirit for, from what we had seen, I felt sure that if a man were prepared to work hard every day he could finish one axe in two or three weeks. But such ridiculous single-minded application to a task is largely a Western characteristic; these people worked only when they felt inclined to do so.

It was an astonishing scene, for as we watched these semi-naked craftsmen, their head-plumes bobbing as they worked, their chants almost drowned by the rush of the river, we were watching life in the Stone Age. But one significant alien detail caught my eye. One man, like his companions in every other respect, was putting the finishing touches to the haft of his axe, not with a stone blade, but with a shining metal knife. If we were watching the Stone Age, we were witnessing one of its last stages. Furthermore, the axes these craftsmen were making had no real utilitarian function. The blades were too thin, they flared too widely, their cutting edge was too finely tapered for them to be really serviceable. If one were used to fell a tree, it would chip and splinter. If it were taken to war, its huge cumbersome counterbalance would prove disastrously unwieldy.

These axes were larger, more flamboyant and more decorative than the stubby, begrimed and workmanlike example with its steel-sharp cutting edge which I had acquired at Kwibun; but to my eyes they were also less beautiful, and without doubt they had no practical value. Splendid though they looked, they had become non-functional and effete. These men were now only making them to serve ritual purposes – for display at sing-sings or perhaps, since custom sometimes demanded it, for inclusion in a bride-price.

Two things may happen to the stone axes in the future. As the craftsmen realize that their products need no longer be serviceable, they may employ softer and more easily worked stone and tend to make the blades even more ornamental; or else tribal traditions, already weakened by the teaching of missionaries, will no longer insist on the presence of axes at ritual occasions. When either happens, the Stone Age in this part of New Guinea will be over.

That night, as we sat in the house-kiap, a panting tribesman appeared on the veranda with a message. To my joy, he had brought it in a cleft stick. I had hardly dared to believe that such a custom, so reminiscent of the old-style adventure stories, could still exist, but the New Guinea native has no pockets in his scanty costume, nowhere to keep a letter uncrumpled and unsoiled, and the cleft stick still provides the best solution.

I undid the binding at the top and extracted the letter. It was from Barry. He had finished his work at Tabibuga and would join us the next day.

I called Turnim-talk in from the veranda, and explained that we should be staying in Menjim for one more day when the kiap would arrive. Now that I had seen the 'stone-akis' I was anxious to see 'kumul e go sing-sing long diwai'. (Since we had been travelling without any Europeans our pidgin of necessity had improved and 'diwai', meaning tree, was one of my more recently acquired words.) I emphasized that we would not harm the birds in any way, that we would not shoot them, nor would we attempt to catch them. We wished only to see them and to point our 'box picture' at them. If any man could show us the dancing birds, I would give him a pearl-shell of the finest quality – a 'number-one keena'.

Turnim-talk's eyes sparkled.

'Me savvy,' he said. 'Diwai belong kumul, im e close-to.'

Hardly able to believe our luck, I arranged that he should collect us early the next morning and take us to the tree.

'We no lookim kumul,' I warned. 'We no givim keena.'

Turnim-talk took no risks. He called us not merely at dawn but in the middle of the night, or so it seemed to me as I sleepily pulled on my clothes by the light of a torch. We picked up our cameras and stumbled down the path leading out of the village, our boots clinking unnaturally loudly on the stones. We crossed the river by a fallen tree-trunk and walked up to a plantation of cassava. Faintly in the grey before-dawn light, I could see beyond it a group of casuarina trees.

'Sun i come up,' whispered Turnim-talk. 'Kumul i come sing-sing long diwai.'

We nodded, and wormed our way into the centre of a group of bushes where we set up the camera. Then we settled down to wait. The leaves around us were heavy with dew and I felt cold even though I was wearing a thick jersey.

Slowly, almost imperceptibly, the grey sky brightened. I was impatient for the bird to arrive, but every time I mentioned the possibility, Charles countered by holding up his exposure meter and pointing out that it would in fact be disastrous if the bird came so soon as there was not yet enough light to film it by. At last he grudgingly admitted that if he opened the aperture of his lens to the widest extent (thereby, he did not fail to add, reducing the depth of focus to nothing) there might be just enough light to register a dim image on the film.

As he said this, I heard a bird call which I recognized as being that of a Lesser Bird of Paradise. It came from behind us and I slowly turned round to look for it. There was another call and a flutter drew my eyes to a distant tree in which I could distinguish the vague shape of a bird. It called a third time and flew in a swooping arc above us, its brilliant plumes trailing behind it, and alighted in the casuarinas ahead of us. Maddeningly, it settled in the densest part of the tree's foliage and disappeared from our sight.

It began to call, with a new urgency in its note, while I searched despairingly with my binoculars. For what seemed like an age, the shrieks continued and all we could see was an indeterminate agitation among the leaves. Then there was silence. Abruptly the bird shot from the tree and flew off down the valley.

'T'a's all,' announced Turnim-talk loudly. 'Masta givim one fella number one keena.'

'E no come back?' I asked.

'E no come back, altogether,' he replied with finality.

'Orright. Me givim,' I said. 'Turnim-talk go back long house-kiap. We stop lik-lik.'

Triumphantly, Turnim-talk left us. Miserably we waited for another half-hour in the faint hope that the bird might return. I scanned the trees with my binoculars and in doing so I turned them idly on to a paw-paw growing close by us. To my surprise I found myself looking at two large eyes peering at me through the leaves.

I handed the binoculars to Charles. He could see them also but neither of us could imagine what creature it was that owned them. The bird of paradise would not return now, for the sun was already rising in the sky, so we stood up from our concealment and walked over to the paw-paw to investigate.

I looked up into the tree. Nestling in the top crown of leaves

I saw a white furry creature the size of a cat. It was a cus-cus, one of the most charming of the mammals of New Guinea and a creature I dearly wanted to take back to London. As I watched, he uncurled himself and, blinking myopically, began to clamber down towards me, gripping the trunk with his long curling tail. On his way he encountered a vine twisting round the trunk and stopped to munch a few of the leaves in a contemplative fashion. Then he continued to descend towards me, and for a moment I thought he would walk straight into my hands. So that I should be in a position ready to receive him, I made a slight movement. He whirled round and scampered back up the trunk to the shelter of the leaves.

We had reached an impasse. He would not come down while we stood there, and I could not climb up for the paw-paw was so slender that it would not stand my weight. The only solution was to chop it down. I took out my bush knife and began to do so. The cus-cus reappeared from among the leaves and gravely inspected what I was doing. Soon the tree began to shake with each blow. This the cus-cus did not like, so he descended a little way, and with his tail wound round the trunk and bracing himself with his hind legs, he leaned outwards, clasped the nearby branch of a bush and left the paw-paw altogether. This, though at first sight a clever move, was unwise, for the bush was low and one in which I could clamber myself. I put down my knife and took off my jersey for, in a cowardly way, I much prefer to catch such creatures in a cloth of some sort as I believe it minimizes the chances of being bitten. As I reached up towards him the cus-cus gargled at me in a threatening way and retreated a few inches. The branch supporting him was thin, however, and began to bend under the cus-cus's weight. He could go back no farther. With a swoop of my jersey, I caught him by the back of his neck, unwound his tail and brought him down growling fiercely.

The cus-cus, like all the truly indigenous mammals of New Guinea, is a marsupial and has a pouch like a kangaroo. Its range is widespread for it is found not only in New Guinea, but in northern Australia and in many of the islands of eastern Indonesia. It exists in many different colours. Our capture was unusual in being pure white, the commoner colours being brown or white spotted with orange. He had a moist pink nose, and naked paws, and had coiled his tail like a watch spring. Our joy in having found him temporarily outweighed our disappointment at having failed to see the paradise bird's dance, and we hurried back to the house-kiap to prepare a comfortable cage.

CHAPTER SEVEN

Pygmies and a Prospector

THAT EVENING, Barry arrived at Menjim in a cloud-burst. The monotonous swishing of the rain prevented us from hearing his entrance and we were quite startled when he suddenly appeared and stood, dripping, on the veranda. He brought news which added a further complication to our plans. The night before he had left Tabibuga, he had called Hagen on the radio to report his departure and had been asked by the DC to inspect an airstrip which a gold prospector named Jim MacKinnon had just completed at a place called Kumburuf, on the northern flanks of the Bismarck Mountains. A plane had been chartered to fly over the strip in four days' time and if the pilot saw ground signals indicating that the new strip was serviceable, he would land with a load of stores. The only person qualified to give such a signal was a Government officer and, if Barry were to get there in time to do so, we should all have to leave Menjim the next morning.

As Barry told us all this, the rain continued to hurl itself on the roof of the house-kiap and poured from the eaves so that the windows seemed curtained with a continuous sheet of water. I gloomily contemplated the prospect of marching for several days in such conditions and, in an endeavour to be philosophical, reasoned that it was better that the weather should be bad during a day committed to travelling than during one on which we were trying to film. The logic of this, however, gave me little solace when in the morning we found that it was still raining as hard as ever.

We had waterproof capes with us, but there seemed little point in wearing them for, if we did so, they would not only flap uncomfortably around our legs, but we would become as wet with sweat as we would do if we walked unprotected in the rain. We therefore packed them in the top of our boxes to ensure that, even if the lids leaked, the contents would remain dry. Then we put on jerseys and bravely set out. When we saw the near-naked porters uncomplainingly shouldering the loads in the drenching downpour, however, it was impossible to feel sorry for ourselves, even though I noted, uncharitably, that the carriers' skins were so grimy and greasy that the rain fell off them in silver drops as it does off a bird's feathers.

The march down the Ganz was an easy one for we were travelling downhill and we were able to fall into a rhythmic stride with our heavy, mud-clogged boots swinging like pendulum-bobs. In the late morning the rain stopped and the forest smelt deliciously clean and fresh; the ground was covered with a deep layer of mouldered leaves and was delightfully springy under-foot. We had never travelled in this kind of bush before. The commonest trees were the giant auricaria pines, the enormous trunks of which, as thick and as tall as factory chimneys, rose vertically, untrammelled by branches or creepers until, nearly two hundred feet above the ground, they burgeoned into a crown of monkey-puzzle-like foliage. Some of these living pillars had been blazed with axes to mark the route, and the wounds exuded copious and sweetly fragrant resin. Among the pines grew other trees, some stilted and buttressed with aerial roots, some draped with lianas from which hung epiphytic ferns like ornate chandeliers. Occasionally we saw in the gardens growing on the branches a cascade of vivid orchid blooms. There were birds, too, high in the forest canopy above us. Usually we only heard them — perhaps a shrill, piercing call or, very commonly, the heavy, noisy beating of wings which is characteristic of a hornbill — but occasionally we saw them also. Lesser Birds of Paradise seemed particularly abundant, their sulphur plumes flashing brilliantly as they took to flight ahead of us.

As our clothes dried on our backs, I felt exhilarated and very happy, and the carriers began to sing.

Our line of porters stretched far behind us, for now that Barry had joined us we needed at least a hundred men to carry all our loads. The track to Tumbungi ran down the right side of the valley and for most of the day we had the Ganz River beside and below us as our constant companion, rushing through gorges and tumbling over waterfalls until, as we neared the Jimi River, it slackened its pace and divided into many channels to braid over a wide, boulder-strewn delta at its confluence. Here we waded across it, climbed a low divide on the other side, and then descended steeply to Tumbungi by the side of the Jimi River.

Instead of a village or a hamlet, all we found was a house-kiap and a shelter for porters, standing lonely and deserted in a small clearing. At the river-side grew a giant tree from which a dilapidated suspension bridge of vines sagged across the river to another tree on a rocky bluff fifty yards away on the opposite bank. There was silence but for the buzz of insects, the rippling of the river water, and the faint creak of the bridge as it swayed gently in the wind.

This was the settlement from which Barry had planned to recruit new porters. If we could find no new carriers we should be in trouble, for the Menjim men would almost certainly refuse to carry our baggage any farther. The country across the river belonged to a totally different tribe, the pygmies, and though the Menjim carriers might be persuaded to go into it under the protection of a kiap and his armed policemen, they certainly would not do so if they were to be abandoned in strange and possibly hostile country and had to make their way back home unprotected.

Furthermore, if we induced them to go beyond their own territory, they would not be able to gather bread-fruit, paw-paws or cassava from the forest as they could do if they were in their own tribal area. They would therefore rely entirely on us for food and we had not enough rice to provide for them. We had no alternative but to pay them off.

Barry sat himself on a stool outside the house-kiap and watched impassively as the loads arrived and were checked by the policemen. Wawawi, who was standing by him, suddenly pointed across the river. A small group of people had come out of the forest and were standing by the water's edge looking at us. They were pygmies. Wawawi climbed up to the bridge and crossed to invite them over.

He led them back over the bridge and in comparison with Wawawi, who was six feet tall, they seemed so tiny that it was difficult to believe that they were fully grown. Their leader was a barrel-chested little man, with splinters of bamboo stuck through his nostrils, three on each side, whitening bird skulls hanging from his ears and a hornbill beak slung at the back of his neck. His brown, beardless face was covered with herring-bone stripes of blue-black scars and on his head he had an extraordinary bulbous hat which gave him the appearance of an animated mushroom. Later, when I got to know him better, I was able to examine this hat in more detail. Its top layer was a cloth made from beaten bark

70

fibre and when, at my request, he removed it, I discovered that the substance of the hat was made up of his own hair clippings which had been mixed with red mud and kneaded into his growing hair so that it formed a stiff solid mass. In fact, it was not so much a hat as an irremovable wig, the lower layers of which were still attached organically to his scalp.

He stood rather nervously in front of Barry, shifting uneasily from foot to foot, screwing up his face in a worried effort of comprehension as one of the Menjim men did his best to interpret what Barry was saying.

Barry asked for two things: he wanted to buy food, and he wanted porters to carry our loads onwards. For both he promised to pay well in beads, paint or salt. He added, on our behalf, that if any of the pygmies had tame animals, we would pay well for these also. The pygmy grunted as he listened, and with every nod his wig wobbled on his head and slipped over his eyes, so that he had to push it back into place. We understood from his muttered reply that he would go back across the river and send messages to the rest of his tribe telling them of our requests. More than this he could not do. Barry thanked him, and the little man and his companions, stoutly independent, returned over the bridge.

The next morning, pygmies carrying food began to cross the river and continued to flood into our camp until well into the afternoon. They brought stems of bananas, bread-fruit spitted in dozens on long poles and carried by bandoliers of vines, bundles of sugar-cane, taro, yams, and cassava. Of all the people who came, none was over five feet high and most were only about four foot six. All, men as well as women, wore wigs, some of which were decorated with feathers, leaves, panels of green beetle-shards threaded on bamboo splinters or strips of bark scored with simple geometrical designs. Some of the people had tied round their necks ropes of beads or heavy necklaces of cowrie-shells which proved that even in this remote valley, so far from the sea, there was still a chain of trade routes along which the shells could come from the coast. One man wore a repulsive necklace of mummified fingers.

As the food arrived, the Menjim men built fires and began to cook some of the vegetables. We ourselves took some of the bread-fruit, large oval green objects, the size of footballs, with prickly green rind. We roasted them on a fire for a few minutes and then split them and extracted the numerous white kernels which tasted like chestnuts. They were delicious.

In the afternoon, our first acquaintance reappeared and came to me, carrying over his shoulder a stick on which, struggling to maintain its balance, perched a white yellow-crested cockatoo. I was captivated. It was a hen bird, for her eyes were brown and in a cock they are black. Her eyes also were ringed with a narrow circle of featherless, bright blue skin, a feature which is possessed only by the New Guinea race of cockatoos and does not occur in the almost identical birds which live in Australia. The pygmy set her down and she waddled off to one of the groups of porters seated round a fire and proceeded, with perfect self-confidence and a great deal of success, to beg bread-fruit nuts.

'Barry,' I said, a little nervously, 'I know your loathing of cockatoos, but look at that one over there. She's not let out a single scream so far and she's absolutely tame. Can you imagine a more delightful creature?'

'Well,' he replied, with mock resignation, 'if you really want a galah, I suppose you could have picked one even nastier than that brute. Go on, buy it! Make me the laughing-stock of my cops! I suppose I should be grateful that at least you didn't find her at Tabibuga, so that everyone in the place would see how my rules could be flouted.'

So we traded her for a pearl-shell and Cocky became the least rare, but the most consistently entertaining, member of the menagerie which we took back to London. I assumed that the Zoo would have so many cockatoos that they would not want her and from the first I regarded her as a future pet for my London home. When she did arrive in England, however, I discovered that the Zoo had never possessed a New Guinea Blue-eyed Cockatoo and wanted to have her. But by that time she had wormed her way so deeply into my affections that I could not bring myself to surrender her.

With the addition of Cocky, we had now quite a large collection – the cus-cus, the pythons, fig parrots, a young hornbill which some tribesmen had brought to us earlier – and as I cleaned out the cages, the pygmies clustered round to watch. Each time I relined a cage with clean newspaper and threw away the old sheets, soiled and sodden with droppings, the pygmies pounced on them and carried them away to the riverside, where they gently and carefully washed them clean. Then they dried them over the fires, and that evening I saw them roll some of their native tobacco in the precious paper and sit back, their faces wreathed in smiles of satisfaction, to smoke.

By the next morning nearly a hundred pygmies had congregated on the other side of the river. We could move on. One by one our loads were carried over the swaying bridge, which was so rickety that we dared not risk allowing more than two men and a load on it at one time. Then began the hardest day's march we had so far tackled, up into the Bismarck Mountains.

As evening drew on, we were still trudging wearily up never-ending grass ridges with no sign of human habitation in sight. 'What lies there?' I asked Barry, pointing westward to a cloud-filled valley. 'No one knows,' he replied, 'no one has been there.' The sky looked threatening as the sun sank behind heavy grey clouds which had accumulated over the mountains in the west, so we decided to go no farther and pitched camp on the ridge. Within half an hour Barry's police had cut poles in the bush and built a framework over which they spread the tarpaulins so that they formed a long ridge tent. Then they erected a tall bamboo up which Wawawi hoisted the Australian flag. At sundown, the police put on their best laps and paraded with fixed bayonets so that the colours could be lowered with due ceremony before the wondering gaze of the pygmies.

The next day's march seemed even harder. It was imperative that we reached Kumburuf, the prospector's camp, by nightfall if Barry was to inspect the airstrip before the plane arrived, so we moved as fast as we could with the minimum number of halts. As we crossed the top of the range we entered moss forest. I heard many Paradisea calls, but we could not spare time to search for them and, indeed, I was glad to keep moving for the permanently sodden forest floor was alive with leeches and, if we stopped, they came looping across the ground towards us. Even while we were marching we were not free from them, for if we brushed through low undergrowth a few always fell on our legs and had to be flicked off with the tip of our knives. The porters were as worried by them as we were, but being barefoot they could easily see the loathsome parasites, whereas if we did not notice them within a few minutes of their arrival, they burrowed through our stockings and disappeared inside our boots

73

to fix their jaws painlessly in our skin and suck blood undetected.

The forest, which we had found at first to be fascinating, began to lose some of its charm. We were marching against time. We could not stop to investigate anything. We could do nothing but wearily keep on putting one foot in front of another and to do so, without stumbling over a root or slipping over a boulder and thereby exhausting more of our energy, we had to keep our eyes fixed to the ground.

At our midday halt, Wawawi arrived carrying a large box himself. Some of the pygmies, unhappy at going so far from their own territory, had dropped their loads and disappeared into the bush. Our carrier line was so reduced as a result that many of the remaining men were carrying even heavier burdens than those with which they had started. If they were any more defections, we might well have to abandon some of our gear.

At last we began to descend through the dripping moss forest and down on to the kunai slopes below at the foot of which lay Kumburuf.

Jim MacKinnon came out to meet us. A stout, jovial man with luxuriant curling grey hair, he looked as though he was almost fifty years old, although in fact he told us he was only in his middle thirties. He welcomed us effusively, shaking our hands, clapping us on the back and laughing excitedly. We were the first Europeans he had seen for many months and he was so overjoyed to be speaking English again that he could not stop talking. Words poured from his lips, tumbling over one another. In his excitement, he stammered badly, he never finished a sentence and every other word was either pidgin English or an Australian expletive.

'Come on in, come on in, my dear old ... By golly, I'm blinkin' glad to see you and to ... It's a terrible blinkin' mess in here, but I'm only ... Aw heck, have some bloomin' whisky.'

The barn-like shack he took us into was indeed in something of a mess. The table in the centre was sticky with smears from past meals, littered with half-used cans of butter, jam and condensed milk, and covered with crumbs. On the pile of trek boxes lay a jumble of red trade cloth, old newspapers and knives. Above them on the wooden wall hung a yellowing calendar decorated with a drawing of an improbably developed chorus girl. An unmade camp-bed stood in

74

ne corner; there was nothing on which to sit except a torn
canvas chair and some up-ended wooden boxes; and the whole
place, as we were to discover later, was infested with rats.

Jim's welcome, however, made up for anything that his
house lacked. He was plainly a most generous and kind-
hearted man, and pressed on us everything he had that we
might want – food, blankets, magazines, drink; we had only
to ask and it was ours. He apologized again and again for the
lack of luxury in his shack and explained that he himself was
only really camping in it, for during the past three months he
had been living up at his *place-balus,* his airstrip.

'I'm bloomin' sorry, but she's ...' he stuttered. 'The
bloomin' balus from the coast was supposed to blinkin' drop
he ... After all a blinkin' roller isn't too bloomin' heavy,
is it, Barry? Can't understand it. Pilot's bloomin' nice bloke;
nicest blinkin' bloke as you'll find in the bloomin' territory.
Not his blinkin' fault. But I didn't get me bloomin' roller.
So, you see, Barry, she's not bloomin' good enough. Not
really. Not by a long blinkin' chalk.'

He shook his head sadly.

It appeared that after months of work, clearing bush,
planing off bumps and ridges, and filling in hollows, the airstrip was almost complete. But to make it safe and serviceable it needed compacting with a heavy roller. Jim had
arranged for a charter plane to fly over the strip and drop
such a roller, but it had not arrived on the scheduled day
and by radio he had learned that the roller exceeded in either
weight or size some dimension specified by an air-safety
regulation. By the time this happened, however, his request
for a Patrol Officer to inspect the strip had been passed to
the DC at Hagen and on to Barry. It seemed as though our
visit was unnecessary, for Jim himself believed that the plane
could not land safely on the strip. Nonetheless Barry pointed
out that the plane would be coming over looking for a signal
and that he must go to the strip to make it.

Most of the Tumbungi porters left us the next morning, in
spite of our attempts to persuade them to stay. There seemed
very few people around Kumburuf from whom we could recruit replacements, but Jim said that there would be plenty
about in a day or so.

'They're all off on one of their bloomin' sing-sings,' he
said. 'They're up at the place-balus havin' a hell of a party
piercin' the young kids' blinkin' noses with bats' teeth.'

Because of this news, Charles and I decided to accompany Barry and Jim to the airstrip in case we could film the sing-sing. On the way, Jim told me more about his claim. He had been prospecting for gold for nearly twenty years, at first in the northern territories of Australia and then in New Guinea. Until two years ago, he had never made a strike which produced gold in any quantity, but the fever of prospecting gripped him and he was haunted by the stories of Edie Creek, the enormously rich strike that in the 1920s had turned a few lucky prospectors into millionaires. After each of his unsuccessful trips he had returned to some other job to earn enough money to enable him to go once again into the wilds searching for the gold mine which would make his fortune. At Kumburuf, he believed he had found it.

He had washed gold in small quantities from two parallel creeks running on either side of his shack and he believed that the precious metal was being shed from the ridge which ran between them. He and his partner, who had recently returned to Australia for a few months, had built a long water conduit down the mountain slopes to provide a race for a monitor, a small gold-washing machine, with which he was now extracting an ounce of gold a day. He had now decided that in order to work profitably he needed several more large monitors.

'When we get those in, Dave,' he said to me, leaning on his stick for a rest and wiping his brow. 'When we get those she'll come blinkin' good.'

In order to get them, he had stopped work on the claim itself and had spent the past three months building his place balus so that the new machinery could be flown in. The decision not to drop the roller had been a bitter, almost crushing, disappointment to him.

We reached the airstrip late in the evening, in pouring rain. A few pygmies were standing disconsolately in one of the shelters Jim had built by its side. They were hollow-eyed and exhausted, their cockatoo head-dresses bedraggled and awry, for they had been dancing for three days and three nights. Among them were a few boys, their noses newly pierced and their cheeks and upper lips caked with dried trickles of blood. The sing-sing and ceremony were already over, and for Charles and me the excursion to the airstrip had been pointless. It was no more fruitful for Barry, because not only was the strip too soft to be serviceable but, perhaps

76

because of the bad weather, the plane itself never flew over and the sign, which Barry laid out so carefully in white cloth the next day, remained unread.

Gloomily we walked back to Kumburuf in a steady drizzle to find, when we arrived, that all of our Jimi pygmies had now disappeared. We tried that night to muster some porters but, although the sing-sing was over, few people had yet returned to their homes. In the morning we could assemble no more than thirty, and we had no alternative but to abandon some of our loads. Barry anticipated that he would be returning to the Kumburuf area in a few weeks to carry out a new patrol, so he sorted out the kit that he did not need immediately and stacked it in the prospector's hut.

Jim saw us leave with reluctance. He seemed peculiarly ill-suited to the life he had chosen for he was a man who loved company and conviviality, and we knew, as we walked away, that he was wishing dearly that he could be coming with us.

As we descended the ridge, he yelled after us, 'Sink a dozen bottles of bloomin' beer for me in Lae,' and when, an hour later, I looked back to his but, toy-like on the skyline, I could just distinguish a small white figure still standing by it, watching us go.

*   *   *

That night we pitched camp in the forest by the side of three small huts which stood huddled together by the side of a stream. Our head porter called the place Kukim Sol. Inside the huts, we found a few pygmies sitting around fires which were burning beneath crudely built cauldrons. They were 'cooking salt'. The cauldrons were made of wet, soft mud, lined with banana leaves and built on top of a rough, construction of stones encircling and enclosing the fire. The steaming water in the bowls came from a nearby spring and contained minute traces of dissolved minerals which the pygmies were extracting by slow evaporation. One man showed me a small packet of grey salt wrapped in a leaf. It had taken him over a week to produce and I wondered no longer that many of our porters had been glad to carry heavy loads for many hours to earn a tablespoonful of our own trade salt.

Our porters straggled in, many of them carrying double loads, for once again Wawawi, bringing up the rear, had found abandoned bundles on the trail. As we sat in our tent that evening we realized that more of our carriers might desert

during the night and that then we would be faced with th
choice of abandoning nearly all our cargo – cameras, record
ing gear, film, the birds – or of spending many days in as
sembling more porters and missing our plane. Should we d
that, it might be a matter of weeks before it would be pos
sible for another plane to come and collect us. Help lay a
Aiome, for there the patrol officer, with a station far large
than Tabibuga, could undoubtedly produce several hundre
carriers if we required them. We decided, therefore, that i
the morning Charles and I, with what few carriers remained
should hurry on as fast as we could to Aiome and then sen
back as many porters as possible to collect Barry and the res
of the cargo. It was a solution we reached with reluctance
for there was a risk that Barry might be stranded for severa
days before porters reached him. If that happened he woul
certainly miss the plane on which he was hoping to trave
back with us for a few days' holiday in the Wahgi. Howeve
we calculated that, with luck, we might reach Aiome in a da
and, if we were able to send back porters immediately, Barr
might just arrive at the airstrip a few hours before the plane
This decided, we spent the rest of the evening reducing ou
kit to its absolute minimum.

The march now became a race. We left Barry just afte
dawn, promising to travel as fast as we could. Within tw
hours we had crossed the top of the pass above Kukim So
The porters told us that only one river, the Asai, and one hig
ridge lay between us and Aiome. It seemed that we shoul
reach the station long before nightfall. Jubilantly, we ra
down the kunai slopes, descending several thousand feet t
the Asai River. We arrived on its banks at midday. To ou
horror, we found that the improvised bridge of branches an
lianas which spanned it was derelict or partially washed away
Wawawi cautiously crept along it but suddenly there was
crack. Wawawi jumped hastily back to the bank as the centr
portion slowly hinged over and crashed into the river.

Meanwhile I had been selecting the shallowest part an
gingerly I began to wade across. The water was flowing s
swiftly that when I was only knee-deep I began to feel ver
insecure. By the time water was waist-high, the swollen rive
was snatching and tugging at me so powerfully that I coul
hardly force one foot in front of the other. In taking one ste
my foot slipped on a submerged boulder and, if it had no
been for my staff, I would have been swept away. At last

reached the opposite bank, but my crossing was of no value except to convince me that the pygmies carrying our cameras and film would stand no chance in mid-stream. We had no alternative but to repair the bridge.

The porters, under Wawawi's direction, began felling casuarina trees and gathering lianas to bind the tree-trunks in position. They worked hard, but as the minutes passed I realized that we could not reach Aiome that day.

It took us nearly three hours to make the bridge strong enough to support the carriers, and it was not until the middle of the afternoon that we had all crossed to the other side. At six o'clock we made camp half-way up the divide which lay between us and the Ramu valley. Our tent was pitched beneath a bread-fruit tree and not far away grew pawpaws and bananas. We gathered the fruit gratefully, for the only food we had packed in our drastically reduced baggage was one tin of corned beef and one of baked beans. Darkness fell quickly and abruptly. We had not brought a lamp with us, so we sat down for our meal by the side of a blazing woodfire and ate the meat and beans from the cans with our knives, for we had neither plates, mugs, nor cutlery.

We marched into Aiome the next day at noon. It was civilization: an enormous airstrip, as smooth and as verdant as a bowling green, flanked on either side by a row of spacious villas. As our wild mountain tribesmen strode along the neat gravel paths bordered with low hedges of clipped shrubs, the little Papuan schoolboys in their bright uniform of red loincloths ran in panic across the airstrip to find their mothers. The only two Europeans on the station, a cadet Patrol Officer and a Medical Assistant, welcomed us with hot showers, clean clothes and an enormous meal of steak, and while we relaxed, fifty porters were mustered and sent off to Kukim Sol in charge of one of the station policemen.

To sit once again in a comfortable chair, to drink refrigerator-cold beer, to stroll aimlessly instead of marching against time, all this seemed an incredible luxury. But two thoughts continually thrust themselves into my mind and marred my pleasure: we had deserted Barry and probably robbed him of his chance of a holiday in the Wahgi; and we had not, after all, seen the dance of the paradise birds.

Throughout the next day and late into the evening, Charles and I tried again and again to twist our estimates of marching time to convince ourselves of the possibility of Barry rejoining us before eleven o'clock the next day, when the charter plane was due to arrive. As we reached the conclusion once again that it was simply impossible, Charles lifted up his hand.

'Listen,' he said, 'I thought I heard singing.'

We rushed out into the darkness. Far away on the black silhouette of the mountains we saw two specks of light. We could hardly believe that they could be carried by Barry or his men, and for two hours we watched them as they flickered and slowly came lower. Then they disappeared altogether – whoever it was had entered the patch of forest at the foot of the mountains. At last we could hear clearly a continuous chant and the light suddenly appeared bright and large at the far end of the airstrip. We ran down towards them.

At the head of the column strode Barry. By his side, carrying his loads, were not pygmies, not Aiome men, but tall, grinning Marakas.

'This crowd,' said Barry, 'have caught some snakes for you. They brought them down to Tabibuga and were so fed up when they found that we had left the place days before that they chased after us. They are still so cocky that they reckon they can take on anyone in New Guinea if it comes to a fight and they didn't care tuppence that they were walking through hostile country. When they caught up with me at Kukim Sol the day after you left, I just told 'em to pick up the loads and keep on marching.'

He laughed wearily.

'Just when I had a couple of really good fool-proof murder charges to hang on them, the old bastards turn up trumps like this.'

CHAPTER EIGHT

The Dancing Birds

THE NEXT morning, as we waited for our plane to arrive, I began to worry. The reception on Aiome's radio was so bad that we had been unable to confirm our charter and I found it hard to believe that the verbal arrangements we had made weeks before in the civilized surroundings of Lae would necessarily result in the materialization of an aircraft on this particular day in precisely this remote corner of primitive

New Guinea. I invented for myself numerous fanciful reasons why the plane should not come – perhaps we had made a mistake in counting the days we had spent in the Jimi and day, after all, was not the one we had specified for the rendezvous; maybe the official with whom I had spoken at Lae airport had succumbed to a bad attack of some vicious tropical disease and, before he was taken to hospital, had forgotten to mention our arrangement to his colleagues; or perhaps there were two places called Aiome in New Guinea and at that very moment the plane was flying to the wrong one.

Absurd though I knew these thoughts to be, I felt nonetheless joyously relieved when we heard the faint drone of an engine and saw a tiny speck appear above the Bismarck Mountains. The plane circled the airstrip and landed, and my relief turned again to worry, for it was a very small single-engined machine and seemed far too tiny to be able to carry Barry, Charles and me, all our baggage and equipment, and the collection of animals. The pilot, however, had no such qualms. He glanced cursorily at the loads lined up on the margin of the airstrip and calling for them one at a time, began to pack them systematically into the plane's hold. The snake cage was almost the first he selected and, when he heard what was inside, he asked me to put an extra fastening on the lid, remarking mildly that if, during the flight, a python appeared between his legs, his mind might be distracted from aviating.

In spite of his confidence about his plane's capacity, however, as the last loads went in we could see that it would be a very tight squeeze. The hornbill had to be taken from his large cage and rehoused in a much smaller one to fit in the only remaining space immediately behind my seat, and there was no room whatever for Cocky, so I took her out of her box and let her perch on my lap.

The journey I shall always remember. It was the first time that Cocky displayed to the full her staggering vocal powers, for as the plane's engine roared to full throttle, she erected her yellow crest and emitted a shriek which cut through the thunder of the engine like a knife. She seemed so perturbed that I feared she might take flight on her own account, but she contended herself with fastening her hooked beak into the ball of my thumb until the most frightening moments of the take-off were over. Soon after she had relaxed, the hornbill behind me discovered that the bamboo mesh of his temporary

cage was easily parted, and made me aware of the fact b
delivering a sharp and powerful blow on the back of my ne
with his enormous beak. I was so tightly jammed next
Charles that it was impossible to move out of the bird
range. In desperation I tried to protect myself by hangin
a handkerchief over his cage, but this had no effect whatso
ever and he continued to remind me very forcefully of h
presence throughout the entire journey.

In between preventing Cocky from affectionately nibblin
the pilot's ear and trying to dodge the worst of the hornbill
attacks, I did my best to peer through the window of th
cabin, for we were flying over the country which we ha
traversed so laboriously on foot during the past four week
Never again would green forested ridges, like those which sli
smoothly and quickly below me, represent mere geographic
features. I was now able to appreciate their reality in term
of pouring sweat, of agonizing thirst and of aching muscle
and I could comprehend something of the sheer physic
stamina and imaginative daring which the Leahy brother
and the pioneers like them must have possessed when the
marched for week after week through country such as this o
their great journeys of discovery.

In scarcely more than an hour, we had crossed the Bismarc
Mountains, the Jimi Valley and could see the Wahgi Rive
ahead of us. The plane dropped gently downwards and lande
at Hagen airstrip. There we left Barry to enjoy a few day
holiday at the station, before he marched back to Tabibug
and resumed his lonely and arduous life.

From Hagen, the flight to Nondugl took only a fe
minutes. Frank Pemble-Smith and Fred Shaw Mayer wer
there to greet us, as they had been when we first arrive
several months before, and the warmth of their welcome mad
us feel almost as though we were returning home. That even
ing we told Fred of what we had seen and done in the Jim
In many ways it was a story of success. We had found an
filmed the axe-makers, we had seen the pygmies and we ha
assembled a large collection of animals which, even if it di
not contain some of the birds we had hoped to find, was a
large as we had intended it to be. Indeed, if it had been an
bigger, we should have been unable to get it into the plan
at Aiome. But, in spite of all our efforts, we had failed to se
the dance of the paradise birds.

Fred smiled gently when we told him this.

'In that case,' he said, 'I think you'll be glad to hear what d Garai has got to tell you. He's coming round tonight.'

Garai appeared after supper, flashing his huge white smile d pulling excitedly at his beard.

'Aaah masta, na you i come,' he said, shaking my hand gorously. He was obviously bursting with some tremendous cret. He leaned towards me, his eyes dancing, and whisred hoarsely, 'Me findim, me findim.'

'Wonem Garai find?' I asked.

'Na me findim one fella diwai, kumul i come play long and belong diwai,' Garai replied triumphantly.

For a moment his pidgin baffled me and when I did sort it ut I could hardly believe that I had done so correctly. ould he really be saying that he knew of a 'hand' of a tree n which a paradise bird came to dance, here in Nondugl here every plumed bird was shot as soon as it appeared.

Fred explained.

'When you left for the Jimi,' he said, 'Garai was rather pset that you had not found what you wanted in Nondugl. uite soon afterwards, he discovered that a Count Raggi's ird was coming to dance in a casuarina just by the house of ne of his wives. So he issued strict orders to the wife conerned and told her it was *tambu* for anyone to touch the ird until the 'masta belong box picture' came back. Ever nce then, he's been worried stiff that a poacher will get he poor thing before you photograph it.'

Garai, not understanding a word, continued nodding enhusiastically, his eyes darting from Fred to us and back gain.

'Mind you,' said Fred, looking at Garai reproachfully, 'I m not sure how long the old rascal's own self-control is gong to last. He's a bit hard up at the moment because he's ust bought a new wife and she cost him all the feathers you aw him wearing when you first arrived, as well as a fair umber of his pigs and pearl-shells. There's bound to be ome sing-sing or other due soon, and as he hasn't got anyhing at all for a head-dress, I expect he'll shoot the bird imself as soon as you've filmed it.'

*   *   *

Ve met Garai outside Fred's house at half past five the next norning and together, as dawn was breaking, we walked hrough the dew down the airstrip. In the grey light I saw,

crossing the strip ahead of us, a tribesman carrying a bo
and arrows. My heart missed a beat, for in his other hand h
held the body of a bird. Garai broke into a run, yelling. Th
tribesman turned round and came towards us. I held out m
hand and he gave me the corpse he was carrying. It was
dead Count Raggi's Bird. Its brilliant yellow head floppe
tragically sideways as I took it and I saw that its magnificen
emerald breast feathers were stained and clotted with bloo
The body was still warm; we must have missed seeing th
bird dancing by only a few minutes. As I sadly examined i
my mind numb with disappointment, Garai questioned th
man vociferously. There was a heated argument at the end
which Garai turned to us, all smiles again.

'Orright,' he said.

I could only hope that this meant that the bird was n
Garai's but had been dancing in some other tree. Before
could discover more from Garai, he was walking on down th
path.

At the end of the airstrip the track continued, throug
fields of cassava growing in neat square plots, to Garai's hu
beyond which the ground fell in a heavily wooded slope t
wards the Wahgi River. As we approached his house, Gar
pointed to a casuarina tree growing a few yards from it.

'Diwai belong kumul,' he said.

We looked hard but could see nothing.

'I'll bet that this is where that poor bird was shot,' I mu
tered to Charles in an undertone. As I spoke a loud call ra
from the tree and a fully plumed bird catapulted from th
thick foliage near the top.

'Im! Im!' cried Garai excitedly.

We watched it fly rapidly down into the valley.

'T'a's all,' said Garai with satisfaction. 'Sing-sing i
finis.'

Although we were too late on this occasion at least v
knew exactly in which tree the bird danced and how ear
his display finished. I turned to Garai.

'Orright. Tomorrow-time you-me i come plenty plen
early-time long this-fella diwai. Na we lookim dis fella pidg
makim play, me givim Garai one fella number-one keena.'

That day seemed interminable. My mind kept returni
again and again to the tree at the bottom of the airstrip, for
knew that now we were nearer to seeing the display I ha
dreamed of for so many years, than at any other time sin

84

we had been in New Guinea. We overhauled the recorder and the cameras and loaded them in readiness for the morning and went to bed early. I had set our alarm clock for 3.45 a.m., but I awoke long before it rang. In the pitch dark we fumbled our way out of the house to a small hut near by, where Garai had spent the night. At our third call, Garai emerged, clasping his shoulders in the cold.

The night was cloudless. The crescent moon was floating low in the sky, horns towards the horizon, and above the ragged silhouette of the Kubor Mountains on the opposite side of the valley hung the Southern Cross, glittering like a jewel on velvet. We were nearly at the farther end of the airstrip before the first signs of dawn began to streak the sky away to our left, and as the darkness dwindled a six o'clock beetle began to stridulate loudly in the grass by the side of the path. I looked at the luminous dial of my wrist-watch; the little insect was nearly three-quarters of an hour ahead of its schedule. From the hillsides behind us came the faint sound of a man yodelling as he set out on his day's work and, closer to, a cockerel called. The Wahgi valley ahead was cloaked with a smooth, level blanket of cloud. Slowly the stars faded as we walked through the dew-heavy kunai grass towards Garai's wife's house. Steam was rising from its thatched roof and its low entrance was stopped with a pile of banana leaves. Garai called hoarsely through the wooden walls to rouse the occupants. The leaves were pushed aside from the doorway and an old wizened woman crawled out, followed by two young girls, Garai's daughters, naked except for their belts and aprons. As they stretched and rubbed their eyes, Garai questioned them. Their answers seemed to satisfy him.

'Orright,' he said. 'Kumul i comd lik-lik time.'

The casuarina tree stood only a few yards away, growing in the middle of a small grove of banana palms. With great caution, we crept through the plantation, trying to find a position from which we could get a clear view of the branch on which Garai told us the bird would dance, while at the same time remaining hidden ourselves. Nowhere could we find such a site for, from every angle, the nearer branches of the casuarina crossed in front of the display branch, but when at last we felt we had found the best position available, Charles quietly erected his camera on its stand and screwed into position his largest and most powerful telephoto lens. Meanwhile, I fixed a microphone in the parabolic reflector, a large aluminium bowl with which I hoped to focus the sound of the bird's calls so that I could record them clearly and isolated from the rest of the forest noises, although the bird would be thirty or forty feet away.

By the time we had completed all this, the sky was beginning to lighten rapidly, although the sun was not yet above the horizon. We waited anxiously, hardly daring to move or to whisper to one another. Suddenly, we heard a flutter of wings and a fully plumed Count Raggi's Bird flew up from the valley beyond. He came straight to the casuarina and alighted on a slim branch, stripped bare of twigs and leaves, which grew diagonally upwards from the main trunk. Immediately he began to preen himself, combing with his beak the long gauzy plumes that sprouted from beneath his wings and extended past his tail in a glorious red cloud. Charles's camera whirred, sounding startlingly loud, but the bird took no notice and carefully he continued his toilet until, immaculate at last, he straightened up and shook himself. Then, head held high, he called – a single, loud, raucous note which echoed over the valley. He seemed in no hurry to begin his dance, for he continued to call for nearly a quarter of an hour. By now the sun was just rising and shafts of its light, filtering through the foliage, glinted on his splendid feathers. Two other birds flew up from the valley and settled in other parts of the tree. They were hens, drab brown creatures which, attracted by his calls, had come to witness his dance. He disregarded them, and continued his harsh cries, occasionally preening himself. The hens remained silent, flitting from branch to branch. Once one of them approached too near his dancing ground and, with a flurry of beating wings, he drove her off.

His calls began to increase in frequency, and I carefully adjusted the position of the parabolic reflector until they produced the highest response on the meter of the recorder. Charles crouched behind his camera, his eye to the viewfinder, his finger on the starting button.

With electrifying suddenness, the bird ducked his head and throwing his magnificent plumes over his back, he scuttled down his branch, a tremulous fountain of colour, shrieking passionately. Up and down the branch he danced in a frenzy. After half a minute he seemed to get out of breath, for his shrieks ceased and he danced in silence.

As we watched, enthralled, I remembered that Fred had

told us that, according to the local people, the birds sometimes become so overwrought that they fall off their branches exhausted and can be picked up from the ground before they recover. Now, watching the dance, I was well able to believe that this might indeed happen.

Abruptly the tension snapped and the bird stopped dancing. Unconcernedly he resumed his preening; but after a few minutes he began his dance again. Three times he performed this ecstatic display and twice we were able to change our position in the banana grove to get another view of him. Then, as the rays of the rising sun flooded the tree, his passions seemed to subside and his shrieks changed to a growling bubble. This lasted for a few seconds. Then he opened his wings and glided down to the valley from where he had come. The hens flew after him. The dance was over.

Exultantly, we packed up our equipment. It was the climax of our expedition; at last we had witnessed the whole of the magical, fabled dance of a wild Count Raggi's Bird of Paradise.

*　　　　*　　　　*

Nondugl, however, had yet another thrill in store for us. A cable arrived from Sir Edward Hallstrom, saying that he would present to the London Zoo twenty birds from the aviaries, if we were able to transport them to England. This was a munificent gift and, as Fred caught them and transferred them to travelling cages, we realized that, with the creatures we had already assembled ourselves, we should have the responsibility of caring for the most important collection of New Guinea creatures to go to Britain for many, many years. It included Magnificent, Superb, King, Prince Rudolph's and Princess Stephanie's Birds of Paradise as well as the Little King of Saxony Bird which had never before been taken alive out of Australasia. Nearly all of them were immature males, for it was better that we should take young ones which would grow their plumes in London than older birds which might be nearing the end of their life span.

We had already devised a method of taking the collection out of New Guinea, but it was a lengthy and roundabout one, for immigration laws would not allow us to take them along the most direct route through Australia. Regretfully Charles and I agreed that it would be uneconomic in time and money for us both to return with the birds, so we decided that Charles would fly home as quickly as possible with the equipment and our as yet undeveloped film.

I left with the collection a few days later, in a plane which came to Nondugl and flew me to Rabaul. It was the only part of my return journey which ran to schedule, for in Rabaul I discovered that the cargo boat that was to take me onwards to Hong Kong had been considerably delayed and, instead of being able to transfer the birds directly from the plane to the ship, I was forced to find quarters for them in the town. Luckily, I was able to hire a vacant shop in which to keep them but I was fearful for their health. The birds, having come down from the cool highlands, found the heat of sea-level very oppressive and they all began to pant. Several times each day I hosed down the concrete floor of the shop in order to keep them as cool as possible, and I was very thankful when at last my ship arrived.

The captain was extremely kind and allowed me to stack the cages in a quiet corner of the boat deck, immediately outside his cabin. Neither did he complain when he discovered during the voyage that Cocky and some of the other birds began their raucous chorus at five o'clock in the morning. The ship ploughed steadily past the Philippines and across the China Sea towards Hong Kong, but she arrived too late for me to catch the plane which I had hoped would take me to Singapore. I was stranded, but fortunately, in Hong Kong, I was met by Dr Kenneth Searle, a skilful aviculturist and a great friend of the Zoo, who came to my rescue and gallantly allowed me to keep the collection on his veranda.

My stay in Hong Kong should only have lasted a few days, but once again my plans were thrown into confusion, this time by a typhoon which hit the town on the day I was due to leave it. All the air services were cancelled and eventually it was ten days before I was able to catch a plane to Bangkok which had enough cargo space in its heated, pressurized cabin to accommodate the collection. From Bangkok, after another day's delay, I flew to London in a freight plane which was carrying a load of monkeys. Even this flight was not uneventful, for we unexpectedly had to spend a day in the baking heat of Karachi and just before we landed at Istanbul a small fire broke out on board. Eventually, four weeks after leaving Nondugl, I landed in London.

With immense relief, and not a little pride, I handed over

he menagerie to the London Zoo, and that afternoon I sent
ables to Sir Edward Hallstrom, Fred Shaw Mayer, Frank
Pemble-Smith and Barry Griffin. They were all identical.
Each read: 'Collection arrived London today without single
oss. Many, many thanks.'

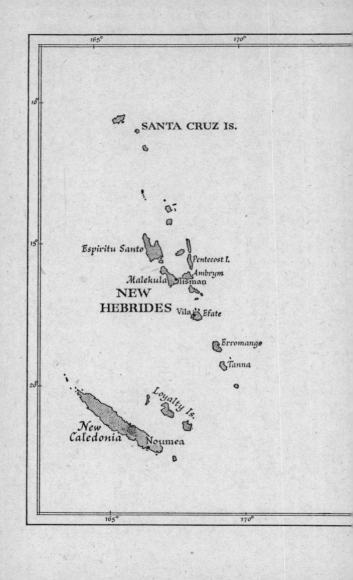

SANTA CRUZ IS.

Espiritu Santo

Pentecost I.

Ambrym

Malekula Tisman

NEW

HEBRIDES Vila Efate

Erromango

Tanna

Loyalty Is.

New
Caledonia Noumea

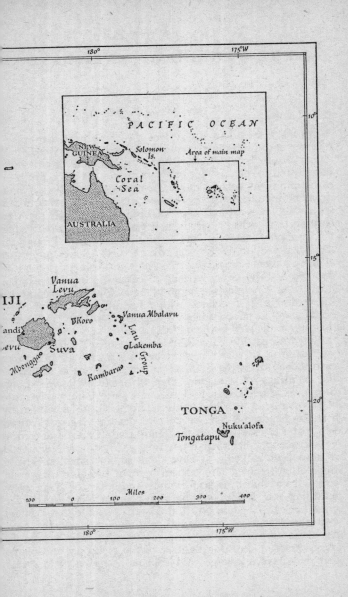

180° 175°W

PACIFIC OCEAN

NEW
GUINEA Solomon
Is. Area of main map

Coral
Sea

AUSTRALIA

10°

15°

Vanua
Levu

IJI

Koro Vanua Mbalavu

andi

evu Suva Lau Group
Lakemba

Mbenggai Kambara

20°

TONGA

Nuku'alofa
Tongatapu

Miles
100 0 100 200 300 400

180° 175°W

PART TWO
THE PEOPLE OF PARADISE

CHAPTER NINE

Return to the Pacific

WHILE I waited in Rabaul for the cargo boat that was t
take me and the birds of paradise westwards across the Sout
China Sea to Hong Kong, I had plenty of time for though
It occurred to me one morning, as I began again the drudger
of cleaning and feeding the birds, that although their roman
tic name matched their glamorous appearance, it was in fac
somewhat inappropriate. It had been bestowed on them b
naturalists who had honestly believed that the birds lived i
the terrestrial paradise. Had those men travelled through th
leech-haunted moss forests, the endless slopes of dust
choking kunai grass, or the mosquito-ridden mangrov
swamps of New Guinea trying to catch the birds alive, the
might well have devised some other less attractive name fo
the creatures. I speculated with relish upon what Jim Ma
Kinnon would have said had I suggested to him that he wa
digging for his gold in the middle of Paradise.

But if an earthly paradise does exist, then I felt I must b
very close to it; surely it must lie only a few hundred mile
east of Rabaul in the South Seas where, if one is to believ
the paintings of Gauguin, the writings of Robert Lou
Stevenson and Herman Melville, and the countless adventur
stories one read as a boy, there lie coral islands inhabited b
a happy handsome carefree people, and blue lagoons fringe
with palm trees waving in the gentle trade winds. I longed t
go and see whether their reputation was justified. Nor woul
it have been difficult to have done so, for small merchar
ships often steamed into Rabaul harbour bringing cargoes c
copra from these magical islands and most of them wer
returning east. But I could not join one, for I had to take th
birds back to London. Nor did it seem possible that I migh
visit the islands on an animal-collecting trip another yea
for these tiny specks of land, scattered thinly across th
largest tract of ocean on the face of the globe, are so isolate
that they have few large wild animals living on them – cer

ainly not enough to justify an expedition of the type that I had just finished. I concluded regretfully that I was then as close to a South Sea island as I was ever likely to be.

The following year, Charles and I set off on our fifth journey together and spent four months in Paraguay looking for armadillos. Soon after our return to London, I was once again considering where our next trip should take us when I received a letter with a Tongan stamp on it. As far as I could recall, I knew no one in Tonga and indeed, apart from the fact that it was ruled by a queen and that it lay somewhere in the Pacific, I knew very little about it. When I opened the letter, I found it was from an anthropologist, Jim Spillius, whom I had known slightly when he was teaching in London. He had written to say that recently Queen Salote, fearful lest the old customs of her kingdom should die and be forgotten as Western ways spread more thoroughly throughout the Pacific, had decided that the most important of them should be recorded in detail before it was too late. In particular, she was anxious that the Royal Kava Ceremony should be filmed. This Spillius described as 'the most important of all Tongan ceremonies in which the Queen herself takes part, which only a few Europeans have ever been permitted to see and which has certainly never been filmed or photographed before'.

Spillius suggested that if the Queen knew that we were willing to make such a film, we might be invited to go to Tonga as Royal guests.

Here was the excuse I needed for a Pacific journey, and as I read the letter, a new purpose for the expedition suggested itself. We would go and look not for animals, but for the old ways of life, the customs and the ceremonials of the South Seas – a journey to film not the birds but the people of Paradise.

The BBC gave their approval to the idea. I replied to Spillius's letter and began to study maps. Tonga, I discovered, lies in the South Seas nearly two thousand miles east of New Guinea and Rabaul. It seemed a pity to go there and not to visit some of the islands that lie between. Why should we not make the journey that I had contemplated in Rabaul two years before?

Compared with the vast empty expanses of its central and eastern parts, the south-west Pacific is relatively thick with islands – the Solomons, New Caledonia, the New Hebrides,

Santa Cruz, the Ellice Islands, Fiji, and Samoa, all of them exciting names. I laboriously devised and regretfully scrapped several itineraries before finally I decided to restrict our journey to three island groups and to plan it so that we should live first with the full-blooded primitive Melanesian people, who inhabit the islands on the westernmost fringes of the Pacific and who are akin to the people whom we had met in New Guinea; then to continue to Fiji, where the people are of mixed racial type, with Melanesian blood predominating; and then finally Tonga to visit a completely new people, the Polynesians.

This settled, I had next to select which of the many Melanesian islands we should visit. Eventually I decided on the New Hebrides, for on one of the islands in the group, Pentecost, there is still practised what must be one of the most dramatic and spectacular ceremonies in the whole of the Pacific, during which men with vines tied to their ankles dive headfirst from a tower a hundred feet high. From correspondence and cables with British Government officials in the New Hebrides it seemed that there was every chance of our being able to witness and film this extraordinary ceremony.

Unfortunately, it was not possible for Charles to come on this trip. Instead, I was joined by Geoffrey Mulligan, a cameraman of my own age and a man with a reputation for having an unquenchable appetite for hard work. When I outlined the plans to him, he became as excited as I was by the prospects.

'This jumping ceremony,' he said, drawing deeply on his cigarette, 'we must make sure we really do it justice. Would you like me to try the jump myself, filming as I fall?'

At the time, I thought that he had intended this to be a joke. Later on, when I had worked with him for some time, I discovered that if in fact he had been convinced that he would have got first-class pictures that way, he would probably have done it.

Vila, the capital of the New Hebrides, lies sweltering on the west coast of Efate, an island in the middle of the archipelago. The easiest way to get there is to fly first to the French territory of New Caledonia, which can be reached either from Australia or from Fiji, and then take a small French-owned twin-engined plane which flies twice a week to Vila.

The New Hebrides is administered by an Anglo-French Condominium which was set up in 1909. Before that date here had been no law and no administration. Demonstrations of the white man's power to impress and frighten the fractious and rebellious natives had been limited to a warship shelling the coast for an hour or two. Although both British and French people were living in the islands, running missions and plantations, neither Britain nor France would accept the responsibility of maintaining law and order. But neither would abdicate her right to annex the territory at some later date. The French claimed that the group was a natural appendage of New Caledonia and that in any case the majority of Europeans in the New Hebrides were of French origin. The British, on the other hand, had been the first to set up missions in the islands and the Presbyterians, under the energetic leadership of the Rev John G. Paton, began an active campaign in both Britain and Australia to make sure that the islands were not taken over by a Roman Catholic nation. In 1878, the two powers signed what was called an 'Understanding' which stated that neither would attempt to annex the islands. This however could not be regarded as being a permanent settlement and when Germany began to show signs of interest in the group, something more positive had to be done. So the Condominium was devised. It was publicly described, at its institution, as 'a remarkable and absolutely new experiment in the joint yet separate administration by two great Powers of one area'. This was certainly an accurate statement, but if the purpose of the experiment was to promote an efficient government, then it must be reckoned a failure.

Today both countries, almost in spite of themselves, see themselves as being in competition as they sit, cheek by jowl, in this enervatingly hot corner of the Pacific. Before leaving London, I had talked to a man who had spent some time in the New Hebrides. He was most indignant about the British Residency. 'It's a national scandal,' he said. 'Our Resident has to live in a ramshackle dilapidated slum on a tiny little island in the middle of Vila Harbour, while the French Resident lords it in a luxurious white palace on the top of the hill overlooking the town. Something ought to be done. We are losing face in the Pacific.' Something has been done. When we arrived in Vila, we found that the slum had been demolished and replaced with a most beautiful modern building in natural wood and gaily painted concrete. The French are outraged. It makes their Residency look dingy and dowdy,

they say. It's a national scandal. Something ought to be don[e]
for they are in danger of losing face in the Pacific. In spite [of]
the wholehearted attempts of government officials of bot[h]
nationalities to avoid petty jealousies, this rivalry is carrie[d]
to extraordinary lengths. Accurate measurements had to b[e]
made of the flagpole at each residency to make sure that the[y]
were both of the same height, for it would, of course, hav[e]
dreadful implications if the Tricolor was either higher [or]
lower than the Union Jack. For similar reasons it would b[e]
impossible for the islands to adopt exclusively either a Britis[h]
or a French institution. Thus there are two currencies
francs and Australian pounds; two systems of weights an[d]
measures; two police forces and two medical services. Ever[y]
thing is not doubled, however; some bodies such as the la[w]
courts, are tripled for there is a special Condominium cou[rt]
as well as a British and a French. On the other hand, there [is]
only one bank and it is in keeping with the special Ne[w]
Hebridean brand of nationalistic lunacy that this should b[e]
the French Bank of Indo-China.

Strangely, the people to suffer least from this clums[y]
double-headed administrative machine are the natives them[-]
selves. In some cases they positively benefit, being provide[d]
with some service which would probably have been denie[d]
them had it not been for the spur of competitive prestig[e]
Furthermore, a tribesman who wishes to break the law wit[h]
regard to his labour contract, or who drinks illicit spirit ca[n]
often manage to play off the British and French Distri[ct]
Agents against one another so that he virtually goes free.

Vila, the seat of this curious administration, is even mo[re]
cosmopolitan than one might suspect, for there are people [of]
many more than two or three nationalities to be seen in th[e]
untidy main street which straggles along the waterfront. Th[e]
diagnostic character, the distinctive field mark (to use orn[i-]
thological jargon), which enables you to distinguish betwee[n]
the various Europeans is provided by the short trousers the[y]
wear. If the trousers are exceedingly abbreviated and in som[e]
such colour as tomato or powder blue, then you can b[e]
reasonably sure that the wearer is a Frenchman. If, on th[e]
other hand, the shorts are so long that they flap around an[d]
half conceal the kneecap, and are in a more severe colour suc[h]
as white or navy blue, then the owner is very probabl[y]
English. Intermediate lengths usually indicate either a Ne[w]
Zealander or an Australian.

The Lesser Bird of Paradise

Some of the dancers wore plumes from six different species of birds of par

The headman began a long, shouted oration

We waded across the Ganz River

The bridge across the river at Tumbungi

With Wawawi standing beside him,
Barry questioned the pygmies

One of the pygmies brought u
cockatoo

The cave was strewn with
human bones

A Pentecost land diver plunges down from eighty feet

The blowholes at Kolovai

Nambas, the John Frum
leader

Girls seize the poisoned fish

The kava toko was placed next to the largest pig

The kava being ceremonially mixed

Queen Salote
the first to dr:
the kava

But Europeans are in a minority in the town. There are
many Oriental people, the men with long straight black hair
cut in European style and of such a length that in Europe
they would be considered students or intellectuals. These are
Tonkinese, from Indo-China, whom the French brought to
the territory in 1921 to provide cheap labour for the plantations. There are also Chinese who own several of the stores,
and there are the native peoples themselves, the *indigenes,* as
the French call them. They are Melanesians, with black skins
and fuzzy hair. In many respects they are very African in
appearance, but they seem to lack that supple loose-limbed
grace which many Africans possess even when they have lived
for generations in towns.

We stayed only three days in Vila, for passages had been
booked for us by an immensely helpful official in the British
office, on a copra boat that was sailing for Malekula and
calling at the plantation of a trader named Oscar Newman.
Newman knew the Pentecost people who performed the jump
and it was he who had agreed to introduce us to them.

*   *   *

The *Liero,* the ship which was to take us to Malekula, lay
dozing in the sun by the jetty in Vila harbour. She was being
loaded with a cargo of planks by Melanesian labourers, big
heavily-muscled men, their black skins shiny with sweat,
dressed in shorts and singlets with grimy American-style
peaked caps jammed on top of their frizzy hair. Several large
crates stood on the deck prominently labelled Mallicolo,
which is the French version of Malekula, for in the Condominium twinning extends to the very names of the islands.
Garbage and oil floated on the surface of the harbour but
there was not sufficient filth to cloud the crystal water, to
poison all the coral or to drive away the black sausage-like
sea cucumbers which lay on the bottom, twenty feet down,
between rusting tin cans. Geoff and I sat in the stern waiting
for the loading to finish. It was already an hour past the
official sailing time, but none except us had been so recklessly
optimistic as to suppose that she would leave on schedule. A
shoal of several thousand small silver fish played around her
sides moving with such perfect synchronization that they appeared to be one single protean body, twisting and turning,
dividing and coalescing. Sometimes they swam upwards until
they pocked the surface of the water with a thousand moving

dimples; sometimes they dived deep and lost themselves temporarily among the corals.

At last the timber was all loaded and secured. One by one the sweating dockers clambered off her. The French captain appeared on the bridge and shouted some orders, and the *Liero*, grunting and puffing and squirting water from her bilges, moved away from the jetty.

It was difficult to find anywhere to rest. There were only two passenger cabins. One was occupied by a French planter, his pale, plain wife and their young baby; the other by a tiny match-stick-legged shrivelled Australian with red rimmed eyes and a parboiled complexion, together with his very stout gold-toothed half-caste wife. The ship was blistering in the remorseless sun, which beat on her from a cloudless sky, making every part of the upper deck so hot that even the wood was painful to the touch. The only possible place to sit was beneath the awning in the stern. There were no chairs or benches, however, so Geoff and I lay full length on the deck and dozed.

Towards midday, we sighted the coast of Epi, a bumpy hazy strip on the horizon. The *Liero* crawled towards it, like a snail inching its way over a sheet of blue glass. As we neared the coast, the water shallowed until we could see the coral-studded sea floor, the engines stopped and we lay motionless in unaccustomed quiet. On the coast ahead, we could see a small house half-smothered by the feather duster like coconut palms which surrounded it. The French planter with his wife and child appeared for the first time on deck. She was transformed. Lipstick and rouge enlivened her pale face, she wore a newly ironed silk frock and a smart straw hat with a scarlet ribbon dangling down the back. I gathered from the captain that there was no other European within fifty miles of their plantation. There was no one to appreciate her new frock, her hat and her cosmetics except those of us on the ship.

With a great deal of shouting, the native crew lowered one of the ship's boats and took them and their belongings over to the lonely beach. For two hours, the deck hands unloaded planks and ferried them to the shore. Then the ship began to shake again with the rumble of the engines, the water creamed at her stern and once again we steamed off northwards.

Geoff and I moved down from the deck to the cabin vacated by the French family and spent the night sweating on he hard bunks. We woke at dawn the next morning to find hat we were lying off the southern tip of Malekula. Tisman, Newman's plantation, was some forty miles away on the east oast, but one of his launches had come down here to meet us. The *Liero* herself would eventually call at Tisman, but not or another thirty-six hours, for she had first to visit several laces on the west coast of Malekula to discharge her cargo, o that she might arrive at Newman's plantation with empty olds which could accommodate the several hundred sacks of opra that were waiting for her. We transferred our belongngs to the launch and roared away.

Within a few minutes, the *Liero* was out of sight and we vere travelling up the east coast of Malekula with the hazy olcanic pyramid of Ambrym away on the horizon to the ight. We sat in the hold quivering with the vibration of the ngine, our nostrils full of the reasty corroding stench of the opra with which the launch was normally loaded. The noise rom the engine was deafening and inescapable, battering our ars so that they ached with very real physical pain. As far as could see, there was no silencer or muffler of any kind on he roaring shaking machinery.

Five hours later, we swung into Tisman Bay. Several boats obbed at anchor close by the shore. Others were drawn up n the dazzlingly white beach. Close-set rows of coconut alms covered the hills behind. Newman, a middle-aged and xtremely tough-looking man wearing overalls and a battered rilby hat, stood waiting for us at the head of the beach by a ine of corrugated iron huts. Leaving his boys to unload our aggage, he drove us up in a lorry to his house at the top of he hill. It was a single-storeyed timber building with shuters over the long glassless windows and a spacious veranda unning along the length of the house on each side.

We sat down on the cane chairs for a drink. A coconut ory flew in through the open window, landed heavily on he floor and waddled perkily towards me. It was a very andsome bird with a scarlet chest, a brilliant green back nd, like all the parrot family, a powerful hooked beak. I was bout to bend down to take the endearingly tame creature on ny finger when it suddenly flew at my sandal-shod sockless eet and bit my toe so savagely that it drew blood. Newman aughed with the hearty satisfaction of a joker who sees someone fall on a carefully laid banana skin. Apparently the bird vas completely unmoved by the sight of feet wearing shoes

and socks, but it was always stimulated to violent attack b
naked toes. As we were to discover later, this first encounte
between the bird and a stranger was one of Oscar's eagerl
awaited moments of pleasure.

'Enjoy the ride, boys?' he asked, sitting down with a glas
of iced beer.

'Yes, very much indeed,' I replied untruthfully. 'It's a ver
nice launch. But she's a little on the noisy side, isn't she? I
the muffler broken?'

'Good Lord, no,' replied Oscar. 'In fact it's lying around i
the workshop somewhere almost brand new. The damn thin
worked so well that the engine made nothing but a low purr
ing noise. You could hardly hear it. Well that's no damn goo
in this part of the world. We used to arrive at a landing t
collect some copra and then spend the next couple of hour
yelling our heads off to let the bushies know that we ha
arrived. So we took the muffler off. Now they can hear u
coming while we are still five miles away and they are alway
on the beach to meet us.'

Oscar was born in the New Hebrides, the son of a
Englishman who had planted coconuts on several parts of th
coast of Malekula, but who had never made a financial suc
cess of his ventures and had died in debt. Oscar told us tha
he swore to himself that he would pay off all his father'
debts himself. This he did and now he is reputedly one of th
richest men in the whole of the New Hebrides. Until a yea
or so previously, his wife and his two sons had lived with hir
in the big house at Tisman. Now they have gone down t
Australia, the boys have got married and Oscar is alone. Fo
a long time, Oscar has been saying that he too was going t
leave the New Hebrides and retire. A few months earlier h
had sold the plantation and the chain of trade stores h
owned in the nearby islands to one of the big French tradin
concerns. But no one could believe that Oscar would leav
the New Hebrides for good and so no one was surprised whe
it turned out that he was stopping on in Tisman as manager.

'I'm only doing it to help them out,' he said to us de
fensively. 'The good times for planters are over. I'm fed u
with the place. The sooner I get out of it the happier I sha
be.' It was difficult to know whether to believe him.

At least two or three times a day, Oscar talked by radio t
Vila and to other people throughout the group, givin
weather reports for the sake of the aircraft company an

changing news and gossip. The most regular of his calls and one that he enjoyed the most was to a planter on the neighbouring island of Ambrym named Mitchell. They had been acquainted for at least thirty years, but they never called one another by anything except their surnames. Oscar spoke to Mitchell that evening.

'The *Liero* is arriving tomorrow, Mitchell,' he said. 'She's got some cargo on board for you. I've got to go over to Pentecost with two young pommies from London who have come to film the jumping ceremony. We are going to pay a quick visit to find out exactly when they will jump, but if you like we will deliver your freight on the way.'

'That's kind of you, Newman,' came the faint voice over the radio. 'It's probably the fancy decorations I ordered for the kids' Christmas party. Glad they've turned up in time. See you then. Over and out.'

Oscar switched off the set. 'He's a bonzer bloke, old Mitchell,' he said, 'but a rum one. He gives a Christmas party every year for the kids of the bushies who work on his plantation and takes no end of trouble, hanging paper chains all over his house. Hell of a scholar, he is. His place is stuffed with books. Can't think what he wants with them. Never throws anything away either. He's got rooms at the back of his place stacked full with empty match boxes.'

The next day the *Liero* arrived, took on copra and sailed again for Vila. The day after, we ourselves left Tisman in the launch heading for Ambrym and Pentecost. We sailed eastwards across a choppy sea before we reached the lee of the north-west coast of Ambrym. It is a diamond-shaped island, in the centre of which looms a great volcano. In 1912 it erupted with tremendous force, scattering ash and pumice all over the sea and letting off tremendous detonations. A school and a trading store run by Oscar's father-in-law sank into the sea and disappeared. The coast line now is composed of cliffs of muddy grey volcanic ash, runnelled by the tropical rains and sketchily covered by a thin growth of vegetation like the stubble on an unshaven chin.

Darkness fell while we were still several miles from Mitchell's place. Small yellow lights began to appear on the coast and hills ahead. Oscar took out a torch and signalled with flashes. Almost immediately several of the lights winked back at us.

'Damn fools,' Oscar yelled at me over the roar of the

engine. 'Every time I try to signal to Mitchell to get m
bearings, every coon on the island decides to be chumm
and answer so that I don't know where the hell I am.'

Standing in the stern, his arm over the tiller, leaning out
wards to try and see ahead and shouting instructions mixe
with abuse to the boat boys, Oscar steered his way throug
the reefs thundering in the darkness. At last we reached th
comparative calm of the inshore waters and dropped anchor.

We went ashore by dinghy. Even in the darkness, I coul
see that the beach up which we walked was composed o
black volcanic sand. Mitchell came down to meet us with
paraffin lamp and took us up to his house. He was a smal
gentle white-haired man in his mid-seventies. The big high
ceilinged room into which he led us was no doubt clean in th
sense that it was dusted and swept, yet it was enveloped by a
aura of mould and decay. A few pictures, hanging high o
the wooden walls, were so blackened with mildew that it wa
quite impossible to see what they had once represented. Th
shelves of the two large glass-fronted bookcases that stood b
the wall were thickly dusted with yellowing naphthale
powder to deter insect pests which might attack the fade
books inside. In the centre of the room stood two large de
tables placed side by side. They were heaped with a gre
mound of miscellaneous odds and ends – stacks of magazine
curling papers, bundles of chickens' feathers, sheaves
pencils, empty jam jars, odd lengths of electrical flex, an
miscellaneous pieces of engine castings. Mitchell looked at
in a reproachful way. 'Hell and blazes,' he said mildly, 'the
are some cigarettes somewhere there. Do either of you you
fellers smoke?'

'Now Mitchell,' said Oscar, 'don't you go and poison the
pommies with your rotten cigarettes. They stink so bad th
even the bushies won't smoke them.'

'Crumbs,' replied Mitchell, looking at Oscar from benea
his white eyebrows, 'you can talk. There ought to be a la
against people *giving away* the rubbish that you sell in yo
store.' He continued rummaging in the pile on the desk a
at last produced an unfamiliar-looking packet of cigarettes.

'Now, fellers,' he said handing them to me, 'see if you do
think those aren't just about the best smoke that you ha
ever had.'

I took one and lit it. It was so damp that I had considera
difficulty in getting it to light at all. When at last I manag

102

draw a lungful of smoke, its rank mouldy taste made me choke.

Mitchell looked at me solicitously. 'I was afraid so,' he said, 'It's too good for you. You young fellers have very odd taste these days. Those are the best English cigarettes you can get. Several crates of them were shipped up to me in 1939 by mistake and what with the war and one thing and another I never managed to send them back. To be honest they've never really caught on with the natives and, of course, the Australians around here don't know a good cigarette from a bad one. I thought,' he added sadly, 'that a couple of chaps out from the old country would be just the people to appreciate really good quality cigarettes like these and I'd have been prepared to cut a little off the price if you had given me a wholesale order.'

Oscar rocked with laughter. 'You'll never flog those rotten things, Mitchell. You had better throw them into the sea. And anyway, how much longer do we have to wait for a cup of tea?'

Mitchell retreated to the kitchen, saying that his native servants had all gone out for the evening. He soon reappeared with some tinned meat and a tin of peaches. As we ate, the two planters exchanged their news, talked gloomily about copra prices, although they were at the time almost as high as they had ever been, and ribbed one another with enthusiasm.

Oscar carefully wiped his plate clean with a piece of bread and smacked his lips. 'Well, Mitchell,' he said appreciatively, 'if that's the best you can do by way of tucker, I reckon we'll leave right away. I couldn't abide the thought of having to have breakfast with you. I'll call you on the radio when I get back to Tisman.' He clapped his hat on his head and together we went down to the boat.

That night, we sailed across the eight miles of rough water that separates the northern point of Ambrym from the southernmost tip of Pentecost. We anchored in a bay, spread sacks in the hold of the launch, and, doing our best to ignore the stench of copra, went to sleep.

We were woken, just before sunrise, by the sound of a puttering little launch which came bobbing across the water towards us in the grey light of dawn. At her tiller stood a short fat man, an Uncle Remus-like figure with a straw hat on the back of his head and a white woolly beard running around his chin from ear to ear. Skilfully he brought his boat alongside ours and with surprising agility, hopped on board. Although he was certainly very corpulent, he was not flabby but taut like a balloon inflated to the point of bursting. Osca greeted him boisterously in pidgin and then introduced him to us.

'This is Wall,' he said. 'He's chief of one of the village up the coast and he's the chap who will introduce us to th jokers who are going to do the jump. How's it going, Wall?'

'Plenty good Masta Oscar,' said Wall. 'Six day time, in makim jump.'

This was sooner than we had expected, and as we wante to spend one or two days filming the preparations for th jump, there seemed little point in Geoff or I returning t Tisman before the ceremony. On the other hand, we had no come prepared for a stay.

'I can't stay with you boys,' said Oscar. 'I've got work t do back at Tisman, but I reckon you'll be OK. There ar some tins of tucker somewhere in the hold which you ca have and I guess you'll be able to get some yams and coco nuts from the bushies, so you won't starve. Can you fix 'e up with some place to sleep, Wall?'

Wall grinned and nodded.

A quarter of an hour later, Wall, Geoff, and I were stand ing on the beach beside a small pile of tinned food and ou photographic equipment and Oscar, having promised h would return in time for the ceremony, was sailing out of th bay on his way back to Tisman.

CHAPTER TEN

The Tusked Pigs

THE BEACH on which we had landed stretched for over mile in an unbroken graceful curve. Behind it, almost hidde in the thick bush, stood a few huts strung in a discontinuo line along the length of the bay. Wall led us to a particularl small hovel standing by itself beneath a large pandanus tr on the bank of a sluggish stream. It was derelict, its thatc sodden and sagging into holes.

' 'Im,' said Wall. 'House belong you.'

By now some of the people who lived in the other huts ha gathered round and were sitting on their haunches gravel

104

and unabashedly inspecting us. Most of them wore heavily patched shorts, a few were naked except for a *nambas,* the traditional type of loin-cloth which is abbreviated well beyond the bounds of decency. Wall began to organize them into repairing the hut for us. Some he sent to gather leaves for new thatch, some to cut saplings with which to build an extra portico on the front. This he had decided was a necessary addition in order to prevent rain from beating directly into the open door. Within an hour, the hut was beginning to look quite habitable. We constructed a rough table in the portico on which we stacked the tins of food and our enamel plates. Inside the main hut itself, which measured only ten feet by eight feet, we built a platform of split bamboo to serve as a bed. We made it as broad as possible so that we could both sleep on it side by side, for there was no room for the luxury of two separate ones. We hung up our bag of sugar from a string in the corner in vain attempt to keep it away from the swarming ants. When all was finished, Wall sent a boy up the palm tree that grew outside to gather some coconuts, and the three of us sat on the hard bed, drank the fizzy milk from the green coconuts and surveyed our new home with considerable satisfaction.

Wall wiped his mouth on the back of his hand, beamed, heaved himself on to his feet, and shook us both solemnly by the hand.

'Me go now,' he said, 'Good arpi-noon.' He strode down the beach, back to his boat, and pushed her out through the waves.

That afternoon, we forded the stream by our hut and walked inland along the narrow muddy track that led to the jumping ground. It wound between the strutted pandanus trunks and the smooth boles of palms and then began to climb steeply through dense wet bush. A quarter of a mile up the steep hillside we reached a clearing half the size of a football pitch. At the highest point there stood a single isolated tree, lopped of its branches, around which had been built a scaffold of poles. Already this drunken-looking construction rose some fifty feet into the air and high up in the girders at the top, some twenty men, singing at the tops of their voices, were busy adding further storeys. Others sat on the timbers nearer the ground splitting lianas to serve as lashings, while yet another party were busily grubbing up the stumps of trees from the ground at the foot of the tower.

We spent the rest of that day with the tower builders. At first my attempts to talk with them were not very successful, for I tried to use the New Guinea pidgin I had learned two years earlier. They found this quite incomprehensible. Listening to their own speech, however, I found that it was much simpler than the New Guinea version. They did not use 'fella' at all and employed very few words that were not, at least originally, English. Once I had appreciated this, I was able to make myself understood, though still the intonation and syntax was sufficiently strange to prevent full communication.

They told me that the jumping ceremony would take place in exactly six days' time – which confirmed what Wall had said. I was surprised at this consistency – it is not every unlettered people who place such emphasis on punctuality – but it was clear that the timing of the ceremony was of considerable importance to them.

Two days later, Wall's little launch reappeared around the rocky headland that marked the western end of the bay. He waded ashore carrying a large parcel wrapped in newspaper.

'More better kai-kai,' he said, presenting it to us. I unpacked it and found six square loaves of bread and six bottles of anonymous fizzy lemonade. He had bought both bread and bottles from a trade store some twenty miles up the coast to which he had just delivered a load of copra. We were very touched and very grateful, particularly for the lemonade, for the only liquid we had had to drink – apart from coconut milk – came from the muddy stream through which we and every man who went to the jumping ground waded several times a day.

As night fell, we sat by the embers of our casuarina wood fire talking with Wall. I asked him especially about the old customs and the old ways 'belong time before'. Wall himself was a Christian and apt to sound a little patronizing toward those who still practised the old tribal religion. He called them 'people belong darkness'. All the villages in Pentecost except three were now missionized, he said, but across the strait, in Ambrym, there were still many pagans. He described their villages and their dancing grounds and said that in the centre of many of them there still stood 'tam-tam' got face'. From what I could gather these sounded like the magnificent sculptured log gongs for which parts of the New

ebrides are famous. Most of them have been destroyed and
he few that have reached the civilized world are now the
reasured possessions of museums. It would be worth going a
ong way to see one in its correct setting.

'You savvy place 'e got tam-tam?' I asked.

'Me savvy um,' said Wall emphatically. 'Me savvy um
ood. You like go lookim, me take you tomorrow-time.'

We eagerly accepted his offer and started out early the next
norning. His boat was only about fifteen feet long but Wall
andled her with great skill, thrusting her bows into the heavy
vaves that came racing down the strait so that she reared
teeply upwards and then, as the crest passed beneath her,
wooped downwards into a trough so deeply that blue water
eemed to be overhanging us fore and aft. We landed on the
astern side of the point, some fifteen miles from Mitchell's
plantation, and walked inland. It was extremely hot and Wall
sweated profusely as he led us uphill. Creepers, vines, orchids
and strangler figs clambered up trunks and festooned the
branches. The trees were very varied: casuarinas; wild bananas with broad glossy olive-green leaves; delicate tree ferns
arching their diapered stems upwards to burgeon into a
corona of delicate fronds; and cycads, superficially resembling small tree ferns yet in fact not ferns at all but the most
primitive of all surviving seed-bearing plants with an ancestry as old as the dinosaur's. Occasionally we passed beneath a tall tree which bore directly on its boughs globular
pompons of magenta stamens in such profusion that the
ground beneath was thickly carpeted with the brilliant fallen
blossoms.

Soon we came to some yam gardens planted in a clearing
in the forest and fenced by magnificently built stockades
erected to protect the crops inside from the depredations of
the half-wild pigs that roamed in the bush. A few men, the
first Ambrym pagans we had seen, were working in the fields.
They were wild-looking people with long woolly hair, completely naked except for a wide belt of bark and a nambas.
They straightened up from their work to stare at us as we
went by, answering Wall's cheerful, but rather breathless,
greetings with non-committal grunts. We trudged on through
the narrow lanes between the stockaded fields and then entered the bush once more.

'Where village 'e stop?' I asked.

'Little bit more farther,' Wall panted.

And then suddenly I stepped into the sunlight of a clearing and found myself face to face with the most impressive and startling figure I have ever seen. It was a huge upright log some ten feet tall, slit lengthways for two-thirds of its height and hollowed out inside to form a gong. The top had been carved into a huge head with a deeply cleft sardonically smiling mouth, a jutting chin and gigantic circular eyes.

'Tam-tam 'e got face,' muttered Wall softly.

We stood in silence for several seconds. Then I saw that beyond the gong, which had so far monopolized my attention stood yet another and even bigger figure, shrouded by a screen of withered palm leaves. I walked slowly towards it across the hard bare earth of the clearing. Quietly I drew aside the concealing leaves. The image was horrific. Sculptured from the fibrous trunk of a tree fern, it represented a grotesque naked male figure, with dwarfish hands and arm and a huge face similar to that of the log gong. But whereas the gong had been of plain weathered wood, this image was garishly painted in blue and red, its staring eyes whorled with stripes of alternate colours. On top of it, partly supported by the scaffolding around which the enshrouding leaves were draped, rested a platform so that the idol resembled a barbaric caryatid. Behind it, an inclined ladder of stout pole gave access to the platform. I carefully replaced the leaves in their original position. Geoff pointed to the bush near by. There, half rotted, stood a long rack on which were hung forty or fifty whitening jaw bones of pigs.

The village itself lay only a hundred yards farther on. A few men were lounging by the low squalid huts. One of them, the chief, came forward and greeted us in pidgin. Wall explained who we were. Around the chief's neck, suspended by a grimy strip of cloth, hung a double spiral of yellowing ivory. He had similar rings around each wrist. These I recognized for they have been made famous by the writings of such anthropologists as Deacon, Layard and Harrisson. They were the tusks of pigs.

Pigs, in the New Hebrides, are wealth. If you want to buy a wife, she must be paid for in pigs; if you have committed some crime you can usually redeem yourself by giving pigs to the aggrieved party; and most important of all, pigs are an essential part of the rituals which govern the life of every single member of the community.

All pigs, however, are not of equal value. Sows, in every

land, are almost worthless and with unthinking illogicality
male piglets are commonly slaughtered at birth regardless
the fact that in a few years they could produce offspring.
man – or rather his wife, for it is the women on whom the
burden of caring for the pigs falls – can only properly tend a
limited number of pigs and everyone would rather that his
pigs should be valuable boars. In Espiritu Santo, the island
the north of Malekula, the people value above all else
hermaphrodite pigs – beasts that exhibit characteristics of
both sexes. Such strange creatures do occur in European
strains but only very rarely, perhaps one in a thousand. In
Santo, according to Dr Baker, who made the classic investi-
gation into this extraordinary subject, there are between ten
and twenty intersexes per hundred normal males. These hermaphrodites themselves are sterile and can have no offspring
but there is something in the genetic make-up of the superficially normal pigs of Santo that causes these monstrosities
to be born in relative abundance.

In other islands, however, the hermaphrodites do not occur,
or if they do they are not particularly valued. Instead, the
worth of a male pig is measured by the length and shape of
its tusks, a criterion which is also applied in Santo in evaluat-
ing the intersexes. When the boars are still young, the New
Hebrideans knock out the canine tooth on both sides of the
upper jaw. The lower canine has then nothing on which to
bite, nothing to wear away its biting edge. It therefore grows
upwards unimpeded, circling back and down until when the
pig is seven or eight years old, the tip of the tusk has almost
completed a circle and meets the flesh of the lower jaw. The
pig is now extremely valuable. It would be considered a
bargain if you could buy one for sixty or seventy pounds. But
the tusk continues growing, insistently forcing its point into
the pig's flesh. The poor beast must now be in great pain.
Still the tusk grows, beginning a second spiral deep in the
flesh of the lower jaw, growing alongside its own base still
socketed in the bone. In exceptional cases, the pig may survive for another seven years and the tusk complete the second
circle. It is then so valuable that a man could justifiably ask
almost any price for it. A three-circle tusker is such a treasure
that you might have to pay a fee of one ordinary pig just to
look at it.

A boar loses a great deal of its value if the tusks grow
asymmetrically or if one is damaged. Dead, it is almost

worthless. The circling tusks, when removed from the jaw of the carcass, are regarded merely as bangles to be trade for a pound or two. The owners of valuable boars therefor are in a state of perpetual anxiety lest their pigs, which they are extravagantly tusked must certainly be aged, shoul die and the savings of years vanish.

One such pig was tethered to the corner post of the hous by which we were standing. It lay in a wallow it had ex cavated by itself, its tusks circling on either side of its jaw Obviously they would prevent it from grubbing and foragin for roots as it would normally do, but in any case it wa quite clear that its owner would never allow it to do such thing in case the all-important tusks should be damaged. I was a wretched sickly creature with a scaly skin and hollo flanks.

But it would not be allowed to die. It would be killed. Th supreme function of tusked pigs, the purpose for which the are nursed, sometimes suckled by the women, tended an reared, is to be sacrificed in the rituals that accompany man's rise in community. The New Hebridean society is graded one, with many ranks, each having its own privilege and responsibilities. To enter even the lowest of them a ma must sacrifice many pigs, so many in fact that not everyone able to earn or borrow enough to enable him to do so. T attain the highest rank of all, it may be necessary to kill mar hundreds.

It was just such a ceremony that had been enacted a fe months previously when the great painted idol had been s up on the dancing ground. The chief had announced a fea and on the appointed day had brought all his pigs and stake them out in the clearing. Everyone had assembled and the with the whole village there to witness the act, he had clubbe each one of them, and left them to die in pools of their ow blood. Then began a great feast. The chief provided yan and chickens to supplement the half-cooked flesh of th slaughtered pigs. The tusk-bearing jaw bones were cut fro the carcasses and hung on a rack. After the sacrifice, th people of the village began a dance that was to continu throughout the day and all through the night. The log gor was beaten, its throbbing notes speaking with the voice the ancestors. The villagers, their faces painted, with feathe in their hair, had danced in the clearing until at the clima of the orgy, in wild excitement, the chief had climbed th

110

dder at the back of the newly erected idol to stamp and
osture on the platform above its head.

In the course of that day, he had utterly destroyed the
vings of many years, but in doing so, he had elevated him-
lf to a position where he was deeply respected and almost
eared by the rest of his people, for he was now in communi-
ation with his ancestors and with the gods.

CHAPTER ELEVEN

The Land Divers of Pentecost

N OUR return to Pentecost, we found that the tower was
earing completion. It now stood over eighty feet high and
oked exceedingly unstable, for the upper storeys lacked the
upport of the lopped tree trunk which ran like a rigid spine
o the centre of the lower section. Attempts had been made
o stabilize it by attaching guy ropes of vines to the top and
shing them to the boles of trees at the edge of the clearing,
ut even so the whole edifice swayed alarmingly as the builders
nconcernedly clambered about in it.

Twenty-five men were to make the jump and each of them
ould dive from a separate platform of his own. These were
rranged in tiers up the face of the tower, the lowest only
irty feet above the ground, the highest within a few feet
f the very top. Each consisted of two slim boards bound to
 simple framework by a rough liana which served the
dditional purpose of providing a rough surface to the plat-
orm on which a diver's feet would not slip. They projected
orizontally some eight or nine feet into space, their outer
nds supported by several thin struts. It was clear that these
upports and the lashings securing their lower ends to the
ain platform would have to withstand a very great strain
hen a man jumped and the vines, trailing from his ankles
nd tied to the tower, suddenly whipped tight over the end of
e platform. I asked the builders why they did not use
:outer struts and stronger lashings. They explained that the
upports were made frail purposely; for the platform was
esigned to collapse downwards when the falling diver neared
e ground, thus acting as a shock absorber and lessening the
remendous jolt on the diver's ankles.

The vines that were to serve as safety ropes were gathered

from the forest exactly two days before the ceremony wa
due. Wall told me that this timing was most important, for
they were more than two days old when they were used, the
might have rotted or dried out and so lost their elasticity an
strength. Should that happen, and the vine break, a man coul
be killed. They had to be carefully selected, for only on
species of a particular thickness, length and age was suitabl
Even so, the men did not have to search far, for the vin
hung in profusion from the branches of the forest trees. Me
and boys spent the whole of one day carrying the bundle
vines to the tower. There, other workers tied them to th
main cross-stays of the tower and draped them in pairs ov
the platforms, so that their free ends, those that were event
ally to be tied around the diver's ankles, hung down th
slightly overhanging face of the tower like some monstrou
shock of crinkled hair.

A man on the ground took hold of each pair in turn, shoo
them to make sure that they were not tangled and ran fr
to the platform above, and then trimmed them with his bu
knife to the correct length. His job was a vitally importa
one. If he miscalculated and made the vines too short, the
the diver who used them would be left hanging in mid-a
and would probably pendulum into the tower with bon
breaking force; and if he left them overlong, then a ma
would certainly be killed. Nor was this assessment easy, f
allowance had to be made both for the extra length th
would be given to the vines when the platform collapse
during the dive and for the natural elasticity of the vin
themselves. If I had been due to take part in the ritual, I a
sure that I would have been very careful to check for myse
the length of the vines that I was going to use. Yet althou
many of the men who were working on the tower were
dive the next day and knew the exact platform from whi
they would be jumping, none of them, as far as I could se
bothered to examine his vines.

When the trimming was over, the cut ends were frayed in
tassels, to make it easier to bind them round the diver
ankles, and then bundled and wrapped in leaves to keep the
moist and pliable.

Lastly, teams of men dug over the steep slope at the fo
of the tower, meticulously sifting the earth through the
fingers to make absolutely certain that there were no roots
boulders concealed beneath the surface which could injure

diver as he landed. By the evening of the fifth day after we had first arrived, everything had been completed. The last man had come down from the tower, the last vine had been trimmed and tasselled. The tower stood deserted on the steep hillside, gaunt against the evening sky, like some sinister scaffold.

When the sun rose from the sea the next morning we saw Oscar's boat rocking at anchor in the bay. He came ashore bringing with him three cold chickens, some tinned fruit and two loaves of bread. After we had eaten the best meal we had tasted for several days, we went up to the jumping ground together. The tower was still deserted. During the next hour men, women, and children wandered in one by one and sat themselves at the edge of the clearing. None of them was going to take part in the ceremony. Two of the builders stood at the bottom of the tower keeping watch to prevent anyone walking over the loose soil on which the divers would land. 'No walk 'long dat place,' Wall warned me. ' 'Im, tambu.'

At ten o'clock, we heard distant chanting in the bush. It grew louder and louder until, with dramatic suddenness, a line of people burst from the bush at the back of the tower and began to dance back and forth, chanting loudly. Some of the women wore long skirts of shredded palm leaves and were bare to the waist; others were clothed in the shapeless cotton smocks introduced by the mission. Many of the men had stuck a young palm leaf into the back of their short trousers so that the frond reached to their shoulder-blades. One or two carried sprigs of red croton leaves or a tall spike of scarlet flowers that grew in rush-like thickets in the forest. The dancers stamped up and down across the slope behind the tower in a column six deep. Within a few minutes the ground beneath their feet had been compacted into a series of six parallel terraces of shiny smooth earth.

Unobtrusively, a young boy left the ranks of the dancers and began to climb quickly up the back of the tower. Behind his ear he had tucked a red hibiscus and he had whitened with lime the parting cut in his fuzzy hair. Two older men clambered up behind him. They were relatives and were to act as his assistants in the ritual that was about to be enacted. For the first twenty feet they swung themselves upwards on the horizontal spars that formed a giant ladder up the back of the tower. Then they disappeared into the confused tangle of cross bars, diagonals and verticals that made the interior of the tower look almost solid, and emerged on the front by the side of the lowest platform. One of the elder men pulled up the two vines that hung from the end. The boy stood impassive, his feet on the base of the platform, gripping the uprights of the tower. His assistant crouched by him tying the vines to his ankles. The platform on which they stood was no more than thirty feet up the tower but the boy would inevitably jump outwards and the ground beneath sloped so steeply that the point where he would first touch the earth, some fifteen feet out, was at least forty feet below him.

The fastening of the vines took no more than a couple of minutes. One of the assistants trimmed the loose ends of the knot with his bush knife and then both of them retreated into the tower, leaving the boy alone.

Holding the red croton leaves in his hand, he released his hold in the tower timbers and walked slowly forward along his narrow platform to stand on the very end, one foot placed on each of the two boards that projected from beneath the liana binding. The dancers below and behind him changed their chant to a rhythmic stabbing yell. They stopped their countermarching and all turned to face the tower, holding out their arms straight in front of them; the women adding to the din by whistling piercingly through their teeth.

The boy, alone on the edge of space, raised his hands. Through my binoculars I could see that his lips were moving but if he was calling or chanting, I could not hear him above the shrieks of the dancers. With a slow movement, so as not to disturb his balance, he threw the croton leaves into the air. They spun gently downwards to land on the ground forty feet below. The whistles and yells from the dancers grew increasingly insistent. The boy raised his hands once more and clapped three times above his head. Then with his fists clenched, he crossed his arms over his chest and shut his eyes. Slowly, with his body held stiff, he toppled forward. For what seemed an immensity of time he fell spreadeagled through the air. Then, as he plummeted downwards, the vines around his ankles suddenly whipped tight. There was a loud crack like a gunshot as the struts broke and the platform they had supported fell downwards. His head was no more than a few feet from the ground when the vines, stretched to their limit, snatched him backwards and flung him towards the foot of the tower where he landed on his back in the soft earth.

The two men who had guarded the landing ground rushed

114

orward, and while one of them supported the boy in his arms
he other cut off the vines. The lad scrambled to his feet,
rinning all over his face, and ran back to join the dancers.
he two men dug over the soil where the boy had landed
nd even as they were doing so, another man ran out from
mong the dancers and climbed into the tower.

One by one during the next three hours, the men jumped,
ach diving from a higher platform. Forty, fifty, seventy feet
hey fell. Not all of them were young boys. Geoff and I were
lming and photographing from the top of the tower when an
ld man with hunched shoulders, wrinkled skin and a short
vhite beard, came climbing up nimbly towards us. He stood
n a platform eighty feet up and put on a spirited display of
xuberant gestures before he fell. In the few seconds between
is disappearance into space and the moment when the plat-
orm crashed downwards and the whole tower shook violently,
ve heard a high-pitched cackle. He was laughing even as he
vas tumbling through the air.

But not all the performers enjoyed it as much as he ap-
eared to do. One or two lost their nerve as they stood alone
n the end of their platforms face to face with their test of
ourage. If the urging calls of the dancers failed to make
hem jump, then the two assistants standing in the tower
ehind, added their own peculiar form of persuasion. They
ad brought up with them a small branch from a forest tree
he leaves of which give an extremely painful sting. But they
id not use these on the reluctant diver. Instead they thrashed
hemselves with the leaves, crying out with the pain and yell-
ng to the diver to jump so that they might stop their self-
nflicted punishment.

Only one diver's courage failed him totally. In spite of his
ssistants' cries and the screams of the dancers he retreated
rom the end of his platform. The vines were cut from him
nd he came down the tower, his face tear-stained. Wall told
is that he would have to pay a fine of several pigs before he
ad redeemed himself in the eyes of the community.

It was evening before the last jump of all took place. The
iver stood, a tiny figure silhouetted against the sky, a hun-
lred feet above us. For many minutes, standing erect in per-
ect balance on his platform no more than two feet wide, he
vaved his arms and clapped his hands and threw down croton
eaves. The singers far below him were hoarse, having sung
or many hours, but when at last he leaned into the air and

115

fell in a magnificent swooping curve to the earth, they raised a great shout and, still yelling, dashed from their dancing ground behind the tower across the landing ground to pick him up and carry him off shoulder high. It seemed miraculous that his knees and hip joints could have withstood the shattering jerk that must have come when the vines suddenly snatched him short, yet neither he nor anyone who had taken part in the ceremony that afternoon had been injured in any way.

I puzzled for a long time on what could be the meaning of this spectacular ceremony. Wall, who in his youth had been a famous jumper, told me the story of the ritual's origin.

Many years ago, a man from one of the Pentecost villages discovered that his wife was being unfaithful to him. He tried to catch her in order to beat her, but she ran from him and in an attempt to escape climbed up a palm tree. He climbed after her, and when he reached the top they began to argue.

'Why did you go to another man?' he asked. 'Am I not man enough for you?'

'No,' she said, 'you are a weakling and a coward. You dare not even jump to the ground from here.'

'That is impossible,' he said.

'I can do it,' said the woman.

'Then if you do it, so will I. Let us jump together.'

So they jumped. The wife had taken the precaution of tying the end of one of the palm leaves to her ankles so that she came to no harm, but the man was killed. The other men of the village were greatly humiliated that one of their sex should have been tricked by a woman. So they built a tower many times highter than a palm tree and started the jumping ceremony to prove to the women who came to watch them that they are after all the superior sex.

As literal truth, Wall's story was hardly convincing and I was not able to collect enough evidence to speculate responsibly as to its symbolic meaning, if indeed it had one. I asked jumper after jumper why he risked his life in the leap. One man said that he did so because it made him feel better; another amplified this by saying that if ever he had pain in his stomach or a cold in his head, the jump was an unfailing cure. One to two said that they jumped because they positively enjoyed it. Most said simply that they did so because it was 'custom belong dis place'.

I had one clue, however, to a deeper meaning. During the

eremony I had noticed that one of the women standing a
ew yards from me was nursing in her arms something which
took to be a baby. She watched one youth particularly
ttentively, and when he fell and swung uninjured, she
xultantly threw away the bundle in her arms. It was nothing
ore than a piece of cloth. Wall told me that the diver was
er son and that the bundle was 'all same like baby'. Perhaps
he ritual was an ordeal through which adolescents had to
ass before they entered the estate of manhood, and as the
oy performed it, so his mother cast aside the symbol of his
hildhood to proclaim to the world that her baby no longer
xisted and that he had been replaced by the grown man.

If this were indeed the truth, and it seemed to match as-
ects of the story of the ceremony's origin, then one would
xpect that only young boys would perform the jump. In
orroboration, one woman said that in 'time belong before' a
an jumped only once and then it was 'altogedder finis'.
ut if that had been the case it was no longer so, for I knew
hat several of the men whom I had seen diving that after-
oon had taken part in the ceremony several times before.

One thing only was certain. The people themselves had
rgely forgotten the original meaning of their ritual, just as
e have forgotten the original significance of our November
th bonfires. Many centuries before Guy Fawkes, our an-
estors lit fires at the beginning of November, for in early
mes the feast of the dead was celebrated at this time. To-
ay's firework parties are almost certainly the direct descend-
nts of those ancient pagan rites. We still retain the custom
ot because of its origin, nor because we wish to celebrate the
elivery of Parliament from the Gunpowder Plot, but simply
ecause we enjoy it. I suspect the story of the unfaithful wife
as little more relevance to the origin of the Pentecost jump
han the story of Guy Fawkes has to the origin of November
onfires, and I would guess that the Pentecost people con-
inue their ritual for rather the same reasons as we continue
urs – because it is an exciting and enjoyable occasion and
ecause it is 'custom belong dis place'.

CHAPTER TWELVE

Cargo Cult

FROM PENTECOST and Malekula, we returned south t
Vila. There we managed to get berths on a small vesse
owned by the Condominium and optimistically named b
them the *Concorde*, which was bound for the island of Tanna
one hundred and forty miles to the south. Tanna might b
considered to be the last island in the group to attract anyon
hoping to find the old ways of life untouched by outsid
influences, for it was the first of all the New Hebrides to b
visited by missionaries, and since then it has been the scen
of energetic and courageous work by the Presbyterian churcl
On November 19, 1839, the Reverend John Williams, in th
mission ship *Camden,* called at Tanna and put ashore thre
Christian Samoan teachers whose task it was to prepare th
way for European missionaries. Williams himself sailed on t
the nearby island of Erromango where he landed the next da
Within a few hours of setting foot on shore, he and his con
panion, James Harris were murdered by the tribesmen. I
was a year before another ship from the London Missionar
Society called at Tanna. Unbelievably, the Samoan teacher
had survived, but the relief ship had arrived only just in tim
for they were being held captive by the local people an
would certainly have been slaughtered and eaten within a ver
short time had help not come.

Only two years later, the missionaries tried again. Th
Reverends Turner and Nesbit settled on the island and i
spite of great hostility from the natives they succeeded i
winning enough converts for Turner to be able to compil
and publish in 1845 a Tannese catechism, the first book eve
to be printed in a New Hebridean language.

During the next thirty years, there was continuous missior
ary activity on the island, though progress was depressingl
slow. On Erromango, thirty miles away to the north, fou
more missionaries were murdered and although no lives wer
lost on Tanna, the situation must often have been a des
perately dangerous one. But by the turn of the century, th
missionaries' persistence and bravery had brought their re
wards. Tanna became a show-piece, an example of wha
Christian endeavour could achieve working with the mos

118

difficult and recalcitrant of primitive people. By 1940 there
were Tannese men whose fathers, grandfathers, and great
grandfathers had all been Christians. The mission ran a
flourishing hospital and a well-attended school and most of
the Tannese professed to have deserted their pagan gods for
Christianity. But in that year a new and strange religion
sprang up in the island. The Tannese were in the grip of a
cargo cult – a religion as bizarre as any of the ancient pagan
rites of the New Hebrides. In spite of all that the mission
and the Government can do, it still flourishes and today the
greater part of the once-Christian population of the island
are its followers.

*   *   *

Cargo cults are not restricted to the New Hebrides. They
have arisen independently in many places in the Pacific, in
islands as far apart as Tahiti, three thousand miles away to
the east, the Solomons to the west and the Gilberts in the
north. It was in the Highlands of New Guinea, where there
have been many cargo movements, that I first met a European
who had had first-hand experience of one of these cults. He
was a Lutheran missionary and he described the origins of
these new religions like this.

Before the coming of the European, the peoples of New
Guinea had been living in the Stone Age. The only materials
which they knew were stone, wood and vegetable fibres, and
many of them had not seen even the pottery which is made
by some tribes on the coast. Then suddenly, a strange white
people come to their valleys bringing an abundance of astonishing new objects which they call, in pidgin, 'cargo' – petrol
lamps, plastic combs, radio sets, china tea cups, steel knives
– all of them made from entirely new and wonderful
materials. The tribesmen are astounded and mystified. But
one thing is clear to them: the cargo cannot be of human
origin. The very substances of which these objects are made
do not occur in nature. And by what magic process are they
fashioned? How could you chip or weave or carve such a
thing as a shining enamelled refrigerator? Furthermore, the
white people do not themselves make the cargo – it arrives in
big ships or aeroplanes. There is only one conclusion to be
drawn from all this – the cargo must be of supernatural
origin and be sent by the gods.

But why should it come only to the white man? Presumably because he secretly practises a powerful ritual which persuades the gods to send the cargo to them alone. At first it seems as if the white men are prepared to share this secret for some of them gladly talk about their god. They explain that the old tribal ways are false, that the old effigies must be destroyed. The people believe them and attend the white man's churches. But in spite of this the cargo does not come to them. The natives suspect that they are being deceived. They notice that the religion the missionaries preach is ignored by most of the white men themselves and it follows therefore that these people must be using some other technique to influence the gods. So the natives ask the traders who have these supernatural objects in abundance, how such riches can be obtained. The traders reply that if they want cargo, they must work in the copra plantations, earn money and then they can buy it from the white man's store. But this is not a satisfactory answer, for hard as a native works, he cannot earn sufficient to buy anything except the meanest of the objects that he covets. The falsity of this explanation is also proved by the easily observable fact that the trader does not practise what he preaches, for he himself does no physical work whatever; he merely sits behind a desk shuffling papers.

So the native watches the white men even more closely. Soon he notices that the strangers do many senseless things: they build tall masts with wires attached to them; they sit listening to small boxes that glow with light and emit curious noises and strangled voices; they persuade the local people to dress up in identical clothes, and march up and down – and it would hardly be possible to devise a more useless occupation than that. And then the native realizes that he has stumbled on the answer to the mystery. It is these incomprehensible actions that are the rituals employed by the white man to persuade the gods to send the cargo. If the native wants the cargo, then he too must do these things.

So he erects imitation radio aerials. He puts a white cloth on an improvised table, places a bowl of flowers in the middle and sits around it as he has seen the white people doing. He dresses up in imitation uniforms, improvised from locally made cloth, and marches up and down. In the Highlands of New Guinea, the leaders of one cult claimed that a fleet of silver planes would land in their valley and the people accordingly began to build great store houses to receive the cargo as a ritual to encourage the planes to come. Else where in the island, it was said that a tunnel would open up in the mountain side and columns of lorries would drive out, loaded with material wealth.

The followers of a cult on Ambrym formed themselves into a militia, and set up guards on their villages who questioned travellers on their destination and the reason for their journey, and wrote down the answers in a register. They also set up notices by the road reading 'Halt' and 'Compulsory Stop'. Other people sat talking into empty tin cans, in imitation of radio telephones.

The first of these cults to be recognized sprang up in Fiji in 1885. In 1932, an essentially similar one developed in the Solomon Islands. With the increasing spread of Western materialism through the Pacific, the cults increased in number and frequency. Anthropologists have noted two separate outbreaks in New Caledonia, four in the Solomons, four in Fiji, seven in the New Hebrides, and over fifty in New Guinea, most of them being quite independent and unconnected with one another. The majority of these religions claim that one particular messiah will bring the cargo when the day of the apocalypse arrives.

In Tanna, the first signs of a cult were noticed in 1940. Rumours began to spread of a leader who called himself John Frum and who had spoken to the assembled headmen of villages in the south of the island. He appeared only at night by the flickering light of a fire and was said to be a little man with a high-pitched voice and bleached hair, wearing a coat with shining buttons. And he made strange prophecies. There would be a great cataclysm; the mountains would fall flat and the valleys would be filled; old people would regain their youth and sickness would vanish; the white people would be expelled from the island never to return; and cargo would arrive in great quantity so that everyone would have as much as he wanted. If they wished to hasten the arrival of this day, the people must obey John Frum's orders. The false teachings of the missionaries must be ignored. Some of the old customs which the missionaries had forbidden must be revived to show that the false Christian teaching was rejected. In compliance with these edicts, the people left the mission schools in great numbers.

In 1941, there was a new development. John Frum was said to have prophesied that when the day of the apocalypse arrived he would bring his own coinage stamped with the

121

image of a coconut. The people should therefore rid themselves of the money that had been brought by the white man, for in so doing, they would not only remove the taint of the Europeans, but would hasten the departure of the white traders who surely would not wish to stay on the island when there was no more money to be taken from the natives. The Tannese then began a wild orgy of spending at the stores. People squandered the savings of a lifetime. Some men brought in as much as a hundred pounds, and golden sovereigns reappeared that had last been seen by Europeans in 1912 when they had been used as a reward to local chiefs for signing a treaty of friendship.

By May, the situation had become extremely serious. The mission churches and schools were deserted. Nichol, the dour British agent who had ruled unchallenged on the island since 1916, decided that the time had come for action. He arrested several of the leaders, identified one of them, Manahevi, as John Frum and had him tied to a tree for a day in an attempt to expose him as a perfectly normal human being with no supernatural powers. The prisoners were then sent to Vila where they were tried and imprisoned. People said that Manahevi was in fact only a substitute who had martyred himself in order to protect John Frum and that the real prophet was still in the island.

Soon after this, the first American troops came to the New Hebrides, and established their base at Santo. Stories spread through the islands of the great quantities of cargo that they had brought with them and of their extravagance and generosity. Soon it was being said on Tanna that John Frum was, in fact, King of America. Then came the startling and thrilling news that seemed to corroborate this – a battalion of American Negroes had arrived. Physically they were very similar to the local people – they had the same black skins and fuzzy hair, but there was one staggering difference – they were not poor, but as richly endowed with the cargo as the white soldiers.

Wild excitement overwhelmed Tanna. The day of the apocalypse was imminent. It seemed that everyone was preparing for John Frum's arrival. One of the leaders said that John Frum would be coming from America by aeroplane and hundreds of men began to clear the bush in the centre of the island so that the plane might have an airstrip on which to land. Soon the situation was so bad that Nichol radioed Vila

122

for more police. He also asked that an American officer should be sent to the island to help dispel the false rumours that were being spread.

The American came and talked to the assembled people, explaining that he knew nothing of John Frum. To emphasize his points and to impress the Tannese, he fired a machine-gun at one of the notices erected by John Frum's followers, and shot it to pieces. Many of the people were so frightened that they fled to the bush. The sheds that had been built to receive the cargo were burned down at Nichol's orders, and several of the headmen most active in the movement were arrested and deported.

The missionaries tried to restart the school, but out of a population of 2,500 only fifty children attended. In 1946, John Frum was being spoken of again all over the island. The Tannese raided one of the trade stores and tore down all the price tickets from the goods that were on display. This was done, the people said, on John Frum's explicit orders. Once more, several of the leaders were arrested and exiled.

After this, there was a long period of calm. Very few people, however, thought that the movement was dead. Attendance at the mission school was still very poor, the old pagan rites flourished and there were always stories circulating about John Frum and predictions as to what would happen when he brought the cargo.

In an effort to regain their lost followers the Presbyterian church relaxed some of their more puritanical rules. There was no doubt that the way of life they had ordained for the Tannese was a strict and somewhat joyless one. As early as 1941, soon after the first large-scale rising, one of the missionaries on Tanna had written in his report for Synod, 'We have taken dances from them and have done little to replace them or to meet the problem created by such a loss . . . We have clothed religion in black and sombre garments, rubbed the smile off its face as unseemly, suppressed the instinct to express our feelings dramatically as being evil and brought people to confuse Christianity with so called respectability which is synonymous with drabness . . . We cannot expect to meet with success until we prohibit less and are more positively constructive. We must do all we can to make Christianity native Christianity and allow the Holy Spirit a chance to vitalize the native church instead of trying to force it into moulds.' Now, five years later, an attempt was made to put

123

such thoughts into practice. But it had little effect on attendances at the mission. In 1952, there was a further wave of activity triggered perhaps by a fall in the copra prices, which the Tannese believed had been engineered by the traders to deprive them of even more of the cargo.

The Government, having failed to suppress the movement by arresting and imprisoning the leaders now pursued a different policy. The cult was officially tolerated provided that it did no harm to anyone on the island, and no one's life was endangered. It was hoped that it might die a natural death, when the people found that none of John Frum's prophecies showed any sign of coming true.

It was the chance of witnessing if not the birth, then the very early stages in the development of a new religion, that drew us to Tanna. I hoped that, when we got there, we might be able to meet the leaders of the movement and discover from them how John Frum's orders and prophecies originated, and perhaps to persuade them to describe in detail the actions and appearance of their mysterious leader.

CHAPTER THIRTEEN

John Frum

IT TOOK the best part of a day and a night for our ship the *Concorde,* to sail from Vila to Tanna. She was an antiquated vessel, staffed by an elderly Anglo-French captain, a French engineer with only one arm, and six Melanesian deck hands. As night fell, a strong wind came up, and the *Concorde* began to roll alarmingly. Again and again black water came surging over the stern as one of the heavier waves overtook us. The captain stayed on the bridge with the helmsman, the Melanesians disappeared into the fo'c'sle, and the rest of us tried to sleep in the single cabin. Twice during the night, the one-armed engineer fell out of his bunk and landed with a splintering crash on the table in the middle of the cabin. When he was tipped out for the third time just before dawn, he did not bother to clamber back, but reeled over to the stove in the corner and began to heat up the contents of a gigantic saucepan. Within a few minutes a powerful smell announced that he was cooking a strong rather stale curry. Once or twice, when the ship executed a particularly severe roll, this unappetizing granular mixture slopped over and put out the burner, but the engineer, who seemed unaccountably happy and was whistling to himself without pause, scooped it up, poured it back into the saucepan and relit the gas. The steamy highly spiced odour that rose from it seemed to fill the entire cabin. It was impossible to get any fresh air for had we opened the scuttles the sea would have come flooding in with every roll and lurch of the ship. I lay on my back, bracing myself with my arms and legs against the side of the bunk to avoid falling into the puddles of curry and sea water that sloshed about on the floor. When the engineer, holding the saucepan high in the air, skidded acrobatically to the table and announced that breakfast was served, I found, to my regret, that I was unable to join him.

The *Concorde* dropped anchor in a small reef-enclosed bay at Lenakel on the west coast of Tanna. On the beach to meet us, and to collect the mail and the cargo that we had brought from Vila, stood the British and the French agents, a teacher from the Presbyterian mission school and Bob Paul, an Australian planter who had offered, when we had spoken to him by radio from Vila, to be our host. A tall thin man, with sandy hair, a small moustache and a deceptively mild manner, he owned more land on the island than any other European and was the only one to run a large plantation. For anybody who wished to talk to the Tannese about John Frum, he was the ideal host. To have stayed with a government official or a member of the mission would have branded us as opponents of the cult and we would have had little chance of persuading the local people to speak about their beliefs. Bob Paul, however, had always tried to be non-committal with regard to John Frum, neither disapproving nor encouraging the movement.

'Most unhappy people turn to religion in one form or another,' he said to us. 'The Tannese are extremely unhappy and confused at the moment. Why should we prevent them from trying to develop their own form of religion, so long as they don't interfere with anyone else.'

On one occasion only had Bob taken a hand in their activities, and this was at the time of the latest and most dramatic of all the John Frum risings, the affair of the Tanna Army. Bob told us about it as we sat in his garden by the sea, the blue Pacific creaming into breakers on the reef beyond.

'I first saw the Army when I went over to Sulphur Bay on

the other side of the island to buy copra, and found, to my surprise, a party of men drilling in a clearing close by the village. They were wearing imitation American caps, long trousers tucked into sand boots something after the style of gaiters, and singlets with across the chest the letters TA, standing for Tanna Army, and beneath – USA. They carried very well made bamboo guns carved to resemble an American carbine with a long bamboo bayonet on the end of them. Their drill was quite smart too. Some of the boys had been in the police and had obviously passed on a bit of what they had learned. I didn't pay much attention at the time. They weren't harming anybody.

'Later, however, they became a bit venturesome and started to march round the neighbouring villages scaring the wits out of the rest of the people. No one did anything to stop them, so they became more ambitious and started on a parade round the whole island, passing through every single village, saying that the Army had been founded by John Frum to hasten the day that the cargo would arrive and urging everyone to join them. Wherever they stopped, the locals had to provide pigs and cassava to feed them and there was no doubt at all that any Tannese, who hadn't felt particularly enthusiastic about the movement so far, either joined the ranks pretty quickly or else felt very frightened about what might happen to him.

'A day or so after they had started, I came across the Army marching down the road that leads to the Presbyterian mission. It seemed that they were on their way to parade through the mission and terrorize the few Christian Tannese who still remained there. It was to be the grand finale of their march round the island. I went ahead of them in my truck and warned the missionary. "Well they are not going to come through here, that's certain," he said. So we parked my truck across the road and stood in front of it. About a hundred of them with their bamboo guns and pathetic uniforms came marching towards us. When they got really close, we just told them to get the hell out of it or there would be trouble. Fortunately, they turned back and went home.

'After that the Government thought they had better do something about the situation, so the District Officer and some police boys went down to the Army's headquarters at Sulphur Bay to have the whole thing out with the leaders. When they got there they found that the Army boys had barricaded themselves in and were standing on the other side

126

with guns in their hands — and not bamboo ones but real ones. Well, the District Officer doesn't have any troops himself, only a few police boys, so he cabled to Vila for reinforcements. Actually, things weren't really bad — the boys in Sulphur Bay still let me go in to buy copra even though they refused to admit the District Officer — but if you judged from the hundreds of panicky telegrams that jammed the radio wave-band, you would have thought that we had our backs to the wall. So in case any of my friends in the group who might be listening were getting a little worried, I decided to send a telegram myself. It read "Please send first opportunity two heavy-duty pea-shooters, two bags of peas and one case of putty medals".'

Bob told the story as a joke, but quite clearly any situation in which people start threatening the Government representatives with force is not to be minimized. Eventually the Government did send down troops, and the leaders of the Army were arrested. They were deported, tried and put in gaol in Vila. It might have been that the dummy guns and sham uniforms were just being used for practice in preparation for the day when John Frum would send the real things. It was also at least as probable that these actions were yet another example of the uncomprehending imitation of the white man's activities carried out in the vague muddled belief that it was some form of magic.

Since that time, the movement had not been so active, but it was obviously far from dead and we did not have to walk far from Bob's house to find proof. By the side of the roads in the bush, on headlands by the coast, and on patches of savannah, we found the symbols of the cult — crude wooden crosses, painted red, many of them surrounded by elaborate fences of red stakes. Some were no more than a foot high, others as tall as a man. Scarlet gates were almost as abundant. Their hinges were functional and you could open them and walk through if you wanted to do so, but they had been built in isolation, leading nowhere from nowhere. They reminded me of the gates in our own cities which stand shut beneath a monumental arch while traffic swirls around them — gates that are only opened to allow royalty and their followers to pass through on some great ceremonial occasion.

On the top of a hill, a mile away from his store, Bob showed us a thirty-foot tall bamboo mast. A cross was tied to its top and a palisade had been put up around its base. Some orange flowers in jam jars had been placed at its foot, their freshness proving that they had only recently been placed there and that therefore the mast was still venerated. When they had first built it, the local people had said that it was John Frum's radio mast which they had erected at his order so that he could speak to them and send them messages like those which came over the white man's radio.

As we drove along the slippery earth tracks that ran round the coast and across the centre of the island, we often encountered the Tannese trudging along the road, the women carrying heavy loads of sweet potato or cassava, the men with bush knives in their hands on their way to or from cutting copra in one of the plantations. They looked at us suspiciously and unsmilingly. Several times we stopped and asked one of them about the meaning of a nearby cross or gate. Always the answer was, 'Me no savvy.' Until the people had become more accustomed to our presence and had decided what our motives in visiting the island might be, there was little hope of getting any clear answer to our questions. Bob therefore spread the word through the boys who worked in his trade store that we were neither missionaries nor traders nor government people but merely two men who had heard about John Frum and who wished to discover the truth about him.

After a few days, we felt that the news would have circulated sufficiently widely for it to be worthwhile for us to start visiting the villages. Outside each settlement there is a ceremonial assembly ground called the *namakal*. It is always shaded by a gigantic banyan tree. The huge heavily-leaved boughs, the brown furry aerial roots that hang from them and the interlacing tangle of pillars that surround the trunk give an ominous brooding air to these places. Here, after the day's work has been done, the men of the village assemble to drink kava.

Kava is made from the crushed root of a type of pepper plant, *Piper methysticum*. It is not alcoholic, but it does contain a drug which is said to make you dizzy and unsteady on your legs when it is taken in excess or in a concentrated form. It is drunk in most of the Pacific islands to the east and everywhere it is regarded as being imbued with semi-sacred qualities. In Tanna it is drunk in an extremely strong form and prepared in a primitive fashion long since abandoned in most other parts of the Pacific. Several of the younger men sit and chew the roots, spitting out gobbets of masticated fibres. A mass the size of a man's fist is then put in a strainer made from the fibrous bract of a palm leaf and water poured over it into a coconut shell. The resulting opaque liquid, gritty, and muddy brown, is swallowed in one gulp. Within a few minutes, the drinker becomes moody and irritable. The men sit around in silence. It is strictly forbidden for any women to come to the namakal at this time. Then, as night draws in, the men drift back to their huts one by one.

The drinking of kava was banned by the mission both because of the unhygienic method of preparation and because of its intimate association with many of the ancient pagan rituals. The followers of John Frum have reverted to the practice, not merely because they enjoy the taste and after-effects of kava, but because in drinking it they are making a deliberate act of defiance towards the mission.

Several times we went up to the namakal and sat as un-obtrusively as possible, watching the preparation and drink-ing of the kava. Gradually, we came to know some of the men and talked in pidgin to them about trivialities. On our third visit, I broached, for the first time, the subject of John Frum. I was talking to an elderly sad-faced man named Sam. Fifteen years ago he had been selected by the missionaries, as one of the more intelligent Tannese, to be trained as a teacher, and he had taught for several years in the mission school. He therefore spoke easily understandable English. As we sat on our haunches beneath the banyan, smoking cigar-ettes, Sam spoke of John Frum, quietly and unemphatically.

'One night, nineteen years ago, plenty of the big men were having a meeting, drinkin' kava when John 'e come. 'E talk an' 'e say that by an' by he bring plenty cargo. Then men will be happy and get everything they want and it will be good living.'

'What did he look like, Sam?'

'He white man, tall man, he wear shoes, he wear clothes, but he no speak English, he speak like man Tanna.'

'Did you see him?'

'Me no see 'im, but my brother see 'im.'

Slowly, reluctantly and with dignity, Sam told me more about John Frum. John had told the people to leave the school – 'Presbyterian church 'e no good; missionaries put in more-extra to the word of God.' John had told the people to throw away their money and to kill the cattle that the white

129

man had brought them. Sometimes John lived in America, sometimes he lived in Tanna. But always and again and again, 'John 'e promise true. By an' by, white man 'e go, plenty cargo 'e come, an' everybody very happy.'

'Why has he not come, Sam?'

'Me no savvy. Maybe Government man 'e stop 'im, but 'e come, some time. 'E promise 'e come.'

'But, Sam, it is nineteen years since John say that the cargo will come. He promise and he promise, but still the cargo does not come. Isn't nineteen years a long time to wait?'

Sam lifted his eyes from the ground and looked at me. 'If you can wait two thousand years for Jesus Christ to come an' 'e no come, then I can wait more than nineteen years for John.'

I talked with Sam on several other occasions, but each time, when I questioned him about the precise identity of John, how he moved about, or how he gave his orders, Sam contracted his brows and said 'Me no savvy.' If I pressed him further, he said, 'Nambas, big man belong Sulphur Bay, 'im 'e savvy.'

It was clear, that Sam himself though an ardent follower of the cult, was a disciple and not an innovator. The orders and edicts which he obeyed came from Sulphur Bay. Bob Paul confirmed that this village was indeed the main focus of the movement and told us that Nambas had been one of the chief organizers of the Tanna Army and had been imprisoned for a spell in Vila as a punishment for the part he played. Obviously we should have to go there, but I was anxious that we should not appear too eager to do so and that the news of our activities should have spread there before we made our visit. If we arrived unheralded and unexpectedly, Nambas's immediate reaction might be to deny defensively any intimate knowledge of the current working of the cult. If on the other hand, he knew we were paying attention to less important members of the movement, he might well be eager, from natural vanity, that we should take heed of him.

For several days we continued our journeys round the island. We went to see the missionaries and heard how an attempt was being made to wean the Tannese from their cult by starting a co-operative movement in which the full workings of trading were explained in detail. The people could see how their copra was sold, how much money it fetched and could themselves help to decide what cargo should be ordered from the lands across the sea. 'Look,' the missionaries could say to the followers of the cargo cult, 'our cargo comes. John Frum speaks false for his cargo does not come.'

The idea had only recently been put into action and it was too early to know for certain how far it would be successful.

I talked also to the Roman Catholic priest who had a small mission not far from Lenakel. Compared to the Presbyterians, his influence on the island was so tiny as to be negligible. Two years previously his church and his house had been totally destroyed by a typhoon and a tidal wave. Patiently, he had rebuilt it and continued his work. But his teaching drew little response from the Tannese. Only now, after six years of labour, was he about to baptize his first converts into the Catholic church, and he had only five of them whom he regarded as sufficiently prepared.

In his view, the most serious aspect of the movement was the educational one. 'For the past nineteen years,' he told me, 'hardly any Tannese child has attended school and when they cannot read or do sums, what chance have you of explaining the workings of the modern world to them. The longer the movement continues, the more difficult it will be to cure it.'

Later, he suggested to us that the cult had recently incorporated into its myths Yahuwey, the small but continuously active volcano that dominates the eastern side of Tanna. Even at Lenakel, twelve miles away, we could hear the rumbles of its explosions like distant rolls of thunder and on some days when it was particularly vigorous, everything in Bob's house became covered with a thin veneer of fine grey volcanic ash. To visit it, Geoff and I drove across the island from Lenakel, travelling along a muddy road that had been cut through the lush dank bush. The sound of the eruptions grew louder and louder until we could hear them above the noise of our car's engine. Then I noticed that behind the tree ferns lining the road the bush had been buried by a huge grey dune like some tip from a mine. The road twisted and we suddenly found ourselves in an empty Sahara of volcanic ash. Except on its very edges, where a few stilt-rooted pandanus trees were attempting to establish themselves, this great plain was totally barren and devoid of any living thing. Immediately in front of us, part of it was covered by a shallow blue lake. A mile away, beyond the lake, rose the rounded hump of the volcano itself, a thousand feet high. It was too

131

squat to be graceful and not sufficiently high to be visually impressive, but of its menacing power there was no doubt. Above it hung a sullen yellow brown mushroom of smoke and every few minutes the plain echoed with the sound of muffled explosions deep in its crater.

There were many indications that the followers of John Frum regarded this as a place of special significance. Among the pandanus at the margin of the plain stood several elaborate and solidly constructed gates and crosses, all of them painted scarlet. On the plain itself, we found sticks stuck vertically in the ash a few feet apart and stretching in a meandering serpentine line for half a mile to a gate which had been built on one of the hummocks of an old lava flow. On top of the volcano, we could just distinguish yet another cross.

It took us half an hour to trudge up the steep flanks of the volcano, picking our way through a litter of lava boulders that had been thrown out from the crater. Some had the glassy texture of congealed black toffee. Others resembled lumps of currant dough, granular with white felspar crystals. On this igneous slag-heap, only one thing grew – an orchid which raised on its slender stems pennants of delicate pink flowers. We reached the rim during a moment of relative quiescence, and I peered down into the throat of the volcano. Its sides were clogged and encrusted with ash, like soot in a flue, but I could not see to any great depth for the crater was filled by shifting billows of acrid white smoke. Suddenly there was a shattering explosion of terrifying magnitude and a cannonade of black boulders came rocketing through the smoke high into the air above us. Fortunately, the volcano had fired them vertically so that they fell directly downwards back into the crater, and there was little danger of any of them hitting us. The volcano's repertoire of noises was extremely varied. Sometimes it produced echoing sighs as of gas escaping at high pressure; sometimes electrifying detonations which reverberated around the crater. Most terrifying of all, it occasionally erupted with a long sustained roar like the sound of a gigantic jet engine, which continued for minutes at a time until it seemed that our eardrums must split.

After a quarter of an hour, there was a shift in the wind, the smoke eddied and the whole crater cleared. Six hundred feet below us, I could see at least seven vents glowing red hot. They were not simple holes but irregular gaps in the jumble of lava boulders. When one erupted, which it did

132

quite independently of the others, scarlet spangles of molten lava shot into the air, some of them the size of a small car. They twisted, elongated into spanner-shaped lumps and divided in mid-air until at last they reached their apogee and fell back, to land with an audible thud on the sides of the vent.

On the highest point of the crater's lip, we found the cross. It stood nearly seven feet high. Once it had been red, but the volcanic fumes had corroded the paint and only traces of colour were left. The timbers of which it was made were stout and heavy and the task of carrying them up the steep sides of the volcano must have been a very laborious one. Why the leaders of the John Frum cult should have considered it so important to set up their symbol in this place was a question I hoped to persuade Nambas to answer if we finally managed to meet him in Sulphur Bay.

Perhaps the most impressive of all the John Frum monuments, however, was not this cross, but a trio of crude wooden carvings we saw in a small village that we drove through on our way back to Lenakel.

They stood beneath a special thatched shelter, protected by an encircling fence. On the left squatted a strange rat-like creature with wings sprouting from its shoulders, enclosed by a symbolic square cage. On the right had been placed a model of an aeroplane with four propellers, outsize wheels and a white American star painted on its wings and tail. This surely must have represented the plane which would bring the cargo to the island. In the centre, behind a black unpainted cross, stood an effigy which could only be of John himself. He wore a white belt and a scarlet coat and trousers. His face and hands were white and he stood with his arms outstretched and his right leg lifted behind him in a travesty of a Christian crucifix. The figures were pathetically childish, yet they seemed deeply sinister.

At last we felt that the time was ripe for us to seek out Nambas. We drove from Lenakel to the ash plain around Yahuwey, across it, and then down a grassy track. The huts of Sulphur Bay village were grouped round a large open square in the centre of which stood two tall bamboo masts. This was where the Tanna Army under Nambas's leadership had once paraded and drilled. We drove slowly down one side of this square and parked beneath a gigantic banyan tree. As we got out, the villagers gathered around us. Most of them were dressed in scarlet singlets or shirts. One old man proudly wore at a rakish angle, a battered steel helmet, no doubt a highly prized relic from the American occupation of Santo. The atmosphere was not a friendly or welcoming one, but neither was it overtly hostile. A tall elderly man with greying hair, an aquiline nose and deep-set eyes detached himself from the crowd and walked towards us.

'Me Nambas,' he said.

I introduced Geoff and myself and explained that we had come from across the seas to hear about John Frum, to discover who he was and to find out what message he preached. Could Nambas tell us about him. Nambas looked at me closely, his black eyes narrowed.

'Orright,' he said at last. 'We talk.'

He led me over to the foot of a banyan tree. Geoff, standing by the car, unobtrusively set up his camera. I sat down, put the tape recorder by my side and laid the microphone on the ground. The rest of the villagers clustered around us, anxious to hear what their leader would say. Nambas looked around him haughtily. He obviously felt that there was a need to put on a good performance to confirm his position and authority with his supporters.

'Me savvy you will come,' he said to me loudly. 'John Frum 'e speak me two weeks ago. 'E say two white men 'e come to ask all thing about red cross and John.'

He looked around him triumphantly. As we had gone out of our way to make sure that he knew of our arrival and plans, his news hardly surprised me but his people listening were visibly impressed.

'When John speak you, you see him?' I asked.

'No.' Nambas shook his head and then added, enunciating his words with the greatest care, ' 'E speak me 'long *radio*. Me got special radio belong John.' The Catholic missionary had told me about this radio. According to one of his converts, on appointed evenings an old woman with electrical flex wrapped around her waist would fall into a self-induced trance behind a screen in Nambas's hut and begin to talk gibberish. This Nambas would interpret to his followers, who were listening in the darkened room, as messages from John Frum.

'How often he speak you 'long radio?'

'Every night, every day, 'long morning time, 'long night time. 'E speak me plenty.'

134

'This radio; is it all the same like white man's radio?'

' 'E no like white man's radio,' said Nambas mysteriously. 'E not got wire. 'E radio belong John. John 'e give me because I stop long time in calaboose at Vila for John. 'E give me radio for present.'

'Can I see this radio?'

There was a pause.

'No,' said Nambas foxily.

'Why not?'

'Because John 'e say that no white man look 'im.'

I had pressed him too far. I changed the subject.

'Have you seen John Frum?'

Nambas nodded vigorously. 'Me see him plenty time.'

'What does he look like?'

Nambas jabbed his finger at me. ' 'E look like you. 'E got white face. 'E tall man. 'E live long South America.'

'Did you speak to him?'

'He speak to me many time. He speak to plenty men – more than a hundred.'

'What does he say?'

' 'E speak, by an' by the world turn. Everything will be different. 'E come from South America and bring plenty cargo. An' every man 'e get every thing 'e want.'

'Will the white man get cargo too from John?'

'No,' said Nambas emphatically. 'Cargo come to native boy. John say he cannot give white man cargo because white man 'e got it already.'

'Does John say when he will come?'

' 'E no say *when*; but 'e come,' replied Nambas with quiet confidence. His listeners grunted their agreement.

'Nambas, why you put up red crosses.'

'John 'e say, you makim plenty cross. 'Im 'e mark for John.'

'Why do you put a cross on top of the volcano?'

Nambas leaned forwards towards me his eyes blazing wildly.

'Because *man* stop inside volcano. Many man belong John Frum. Red man, brown man, white man; man belong Tanna, man belong South America, all stop 'long volcano. When time come, man come from volcano and bring cargo.'

'Me walk 'long volcano,' I said. 'Me lookim but me no see man.'

'You no see 'im,' retorted Nambas scornfully. 'Your eye

dark. You no see *anything* inside volcano. But man 'e stop
Me see 'im plenty time.'

Did Nambas believe what he was saying? Was he a mysti
who had visions? Or was he a charlatan who was claiming
special powers so that he could influence his people and
make them do what he wished? I could not tell. If he wer
mad, then he had infected the whole of the island with hi
madness. Certainly it was not going to be possible to dis
cover from him whether or not there had ever been an actua
person named John Frum around whom the stories had de
veloped. Nor, I now realized, did it matter. Nambas was th
high priest of the movement, and historical facts and th
material world had little relevance to his thoughts or hi
pronouncements.

I remembered the explanation of the cults that had bee
given me by the Lutheran missionary in New Guinea. It wa
obviously simplified – none of us, European, or Melanesian
work out our beliefs quite so logically – but nonetheless, i
closely matched the observable facts in Tanna. It seems tha
it is too much to expect a people to make, within the space o
two or three generations, the transition from a Stone Ag
culture to the most advanced material civilization that th
world has ever known without running the risk of their com
plete moral disorientation and mental dislocation.

We had visited Sulphur Bay on a Friday, and Nambas tol
me that John Frum had ordained that on this day each wee
the people should dance to do him honour. As evening came
a group of musicians with guitars, mandolines, and drum
made from tin cans, came moving slowly across the clearin
beneath the banyan, playing as they walked. A group o
women, wearing long grass skirts, surrounded them and be
gan singing stridently. Their song was not an old traditiona
chant but simple and repetitious, clearly derived from th
American popular songs which were played incessantly o
tinny gramophones in the trade-stores to attract customers
The people got to their feet and soon the whole clearing wa
full of the villagers jigging up and down in a mechanica
stilted fashion. One or two of them added to the strangenes
of the scene by collecting from the trunk of the banyan som
small mushroom-like fungus which gave off a brilliant phos
phorescent light. They stuck them on their foreheads and o
their cheeks so that their faces were illuminated by an eeri
green glow. The dance continued monotonously, the song

136

being repeated again and again and the people dancing with a drugging insistent rhythm. Soon, someone would produce some smuggled alcoholic drink and these tragic unhappy people, believing that they were doing honour to their god of materialism, would carouse all night.

CHAPTER FOURTEEN

The Firewalkers of Fiji

FROM THE New Hebrides, we travelled eastwards to Fiji. The journey for the modern traveller is an easy one; you fly from Vila to Noumea in New Caledonia and there join one of the huge four-engined French airliners which land for an hour on their way from Paris to Tahiti. Their next stop east-bound from Noumea, is Fiji's international airport of Nandi, on Viti Levu the largest of the three hundred or so islands in the group.

When we landed there I noticed the signboards read *Nadi*, whereas the printed labels that had been tied to our baggage in Noumea spelt the word *Nandi*. It seemed unlikely that both should be equally correct but then I saw that a large pictorial wall map labelled as *Beqa* an island I had previously read of as *Mbengga* and it was clear that Fijian spelling was not as straightforward as I had imagined.

Its complexities, I discovered, originated in a desire for conciseness and linguistic accuracy on the part of the missionaries who first wrote down the language over a hundred years ago. They noted that there were some common consonants which could only be represented phonetically by two letters, such as *mb*, *nd*, and *ng*. As these were single sounds they decided to allocate single letters to them and in these three cases it was obvious what these letters should be for the simple consonants *b*, *d*, and *g* were not employed at all in Fijian speech. The missionaries therefore used these single letters to represent the more complex sounds. Thus the name of the airport, though pronounced *Nandi*, is written in Fijian spelling, *Nadi*. But then the missionaries went further. There were also two other compound consonants, *ngg* and *th*, and to be logical both of these should also be written as single letters. As neither of the letters *q* or *c* had been used so far, the missionaries employed the first to represent *ngg* and the second *th*. As a result, the island whose name is pronounced

137

Mbengga was written in Fijian spelling as *Beqa*, and *Nggele-thimbi* was set down even less recognizably as *Qelecibi*. Strangers found all this so misleading that eventually, many years later, straightforward phonetic spelling was introduced for use in literature printed for outside consumption. It may not be as neat as the missionaries' version which is still used widely throughout Fiji, but it is more easily comprehended by new-comers to the islands.

The airport of Nandi has been built on the plains near the north-western coast of Viti Levu, but the capital, Suva, lies a hundred and thirty miles away on the shores of a magnificent harbour on the south-east coast. To get from one to the other you must either fly in a small plane or set off on a five-hour drive in a taxi, as we did.

To judge from the country around Nandi, you would suppose that Viti Levu was a dry, barren island, for the plains are arid and the gaunt hills behind largely treeless and covered with dry grass. But this is not typical of the whole of the island, for Fiji lies in the track of the easterly trade winds which bring with them clouds heavy with moisture gathered during their thousand-mile journey over the Pacific. When these meet the high mountain ranges of central Viti Levu, which rise to three thousand feet, they shed their water in torrential rains. As a result the windward, eastern side of the island has an extremely high rainfall during most of the year, while at the same time the leeward side, including Nandi, is often suffering from drought.

This disparity in the climate is reflected to an astonishing degree by the vegetation. Twenty miles along the Suva road from Nandi, you cross the watershed and the hills, which hitherto had been parched yellow, are suddenly clothed with a lush growth of tree-ferns, bamboos, banyans, palms, and Tahitian chestnuts.

Strangely, we passed very few native Fijians – human or animal – as we drove. Nearly all the people were Indians, descendants of immigrants who were brought to the island in large numbers, between 1870 and 1916, to work in the sugar plantations. Today there are 180,000 of them and they out-number even the Fijians themselves. Most still live close to the sugar-cane fields, which are particularly abundant in the Nandi district, and we drove many miles before we saw our first tall muscular fuzzy-haired Fijian looking very con-spicuous among the slight and lithe Indian sugar workers.

Most of the animals we saw were also of foreign descent. But man, since his arrival in the Pacific islands, has added greatly to their fauna and we saw several of his introductions as we drove towards Suva. Semi-wild pigs grubbed in copra plantations, slim rangy creatures whose precise origin is something of a mystery – they were most probably introduced by man himself but when and by whom is uncertain. Several times a more exotic creature scuttled across the road in front of our car – a mongoose. These creatures were imported into Fiji from India in the 1880s to help combat the great numbers of rats which had accidentally been brought to the islands on merchant ships and which had multiplied until vast numbers of them infested the sugar plantations. Within ten years, however, the mongooses had become pests themselves, and though they reduced the rat population, they also began to raid hen roosts and to kill great numbers of the wild birds. Now they are probably the most abundant of all the wild animals.

Even the birds we saw were mostly foreigners. Fiji has quite a large air fauna of its own – it includes a swamp harrier, some beautiful fruit doves and several magnificent parrots but we saw none of these. Instead the commonest bird by the roadside was an Indian one, the mynah, a large, mostly black, creature with a white underside, a broad band of white across its wings and tail, and conspicuous wattles of yellow naked skin around its eyes. Almost every tree and bush seemed to harbour four or five of them and they strutted jauntily by the verges, little frightened by our car. We also saw, though less commonly, yet another Indian immigrant, the red-vented bulbul, a thrush-like creature with a pleasing liquid song. The fields were thronged with settlers from Indonesia – perky Java sparrows with pink bills and immaculate white and black patches in their cheeks, which were originally introduced in the hope that they would reduce some insect pests. We were almost in Suva before I saw my first undeniably Fijian bird. It was one of the most beautiful of all the birds of the Pacific, a tiny finch which, because of its hooked beak, has been misleadingly named a parrot finch. Its body and wings were a brilliant green and its head bright scarlet. When I saw it, I was delighted that I had been lucky enough to catch a glimpse of this gorgeous creature which I assumed to be rare. Later on, in Suva itself, I discovered to my greater joy that I could always find quite a large flock of them on the cricket pitch in the centre of the town, bustling over the turf in search of insects or sitting up in the tall palm trees near by, whistling shrilly.

In Suva we fortunately made two quick alliances, first with the Public Relations Office and then with Broadcasting House. Our friends in both places tactfully told us that two Englishmen without a word of Fijian between them would not only find it very difficult to discover whatever it was that they were looking for in the more rural parts of Fiji, but would certainly, out of ignorance, fail to observe the numerous and complicated rules of Fijian etiquette with results that might well prove disastrous. The obvious solution, they said, was to provide guides, and this they did. Broadcasting House supplied Manu Tupou, a tall handsome Fijian who was one of their roving reporters. Although in his early twenties, he had a great knowledge of the traditions of his own people and this, combined with the fact that he was of noble blood and could claim relationship with many important chiefs, made him an ideal guide for us. Furthermore, his time would not be entirely wasted as far as Broadcasting House was concerned, for while he was with us he could make recordings which he could use in his own Fijian language radio programmes. From the Public Relations Office came Sitiveni Yanggona, a young Fijian also from a chiefly clan, who had relatives in some of the islands we were hoping to visit and who therefore would be an invaluable ambassador. Sitiveni – his name is the Fijian version of Stephen – later proved to be an accomplished guitarist, a talent which among the musical Fijians was almost as good an ambassadorial qualification as being connected with the aristocracy.

One of the ancient rituals that we were hoping to film was that of firewalking. There are two completely different forms of this strange custom practised in Fiji. One of them, however, is not a Fijian but a Hindu ritual which was brought to the islands by the Indians. In this form of the ceremony, the devotees walk barefoot along a trench filled by glowing charcoal. The other version, however, is truly Fijian and this is very different, for the performers walk, not on charcoal, but on huge boulders that have been heated for many hours in a great fire of logs.

Only one tribe in the whole of Fiji performs this type of firewalk and they live on the tiny island of Mbengga, some twenty miles south-west of Suva – the island I had looked for on the airport map and had found spelt in such an unlikely fashion. We could see it from our hotel room as a blue-toothed silhouette on the horizon. Arrangements had been made for us to attend a performance of the ceremony and the four of us, Manu, Sitiveni, Geoff, and myself sailed across to it in a small launch. The island measures no more than five miles across in any direction, but it is very mountainous, its highest peak rising to over a thousand feet, and its shores bounded by rocky cliffs of volcanic lava. We sailed through the sapphire sea, skirting its south coast until we came to a small inlet at the head of which lay the firewalkers' village. Most of the houses, or *mbures,* were built in the traditional Fijian manner, each set on its own platform of coral rock and earth, with reed walls and a roof of shaggy thatch. Conspicuous among them glittered a new corrugated iron church. In between the mbures and along the beach grew numerous tall fruit trees – mangoes, breadfruit, bananas, and coconut palms – and the whole settlement was enclosed on three sides by steep, lushly-green hills.

We walked straight to the main mbure in the centre of the village for there we knew that the chief and the elders of the community would be awaiting us. By custom, we had to present to them a ceremonial gift, a *sevu-sevu,* of a few dried roots of kava which here in Fiji is called *yanggona.* We had already drunk kava with Manu in Suva, so we had some idea of the formalities that would accompany the ceremony.

As we entered the shady coolness of the mbure, we took off our shoes. At the other end, grouped in a half circle, sat the chief, his master of ceremonies and the more senior of the men of the village. We took a few steps inside, the pandanus mats which covered the floor feeling deliciously silky to the soles of our naked feet, and then sat down immediately, for it is impolite to stand in the presence of people who are sitting. Manu now began the presentation of our sevu-sevu.

He placed the kava roots on the floor in front of him, clapped hollow-palmed several times, cleared his throat and made a short speech explaining how small and unworthy the kava was in comparison to the great nobility of the chief to whom it was being presented. Nonetheless it was a symbol, though a poor one, of our respect. He ended by mentioning briefly who we were and why we had come to the village. Then we all clapped in unison and said together, '*Mana e ndina,*' which means 'So be it'. Later on when we were more familiar with this procedure, which was the essential

141

preliminary to every visit, we were able to mutter at several points during both Manu's speech and the one that followed 'Vinaka, vinaka,' which means both 'Hear, hear' and 'Thank you very much', as well as 'Good, good', and is therefore a fairly safe remark to pass at any time and fully in accordance with custom. On this our first presentation of a sevu-sevu, both Geoff and I kept quiet.

The chief, an old man with a wrinkled brown face, made no reply to Manu's speech for that would not have been in keeping with his dignity. This task fell to his master of ceremonies who took the kava as Manu passed it over and, with his hand resting upon it, thanked us for our gift on behalf of his chief, explained how unworthy the village was to be visited by such important people as us, apologized in advance for the wretchedness of the hospitality and concluded by assuring us that though the village was poor, the very best of what they had was at our disposal.

The kava was then handed to one of the men sitting behind the chief who pounded it with an iron bar on a wooden block. A large and elegant four-legged wooden bowl was placed at the head of the circle. The kava pulp was poured into it and the man sitting behind it began to mix the drink, using a bundle of fibres as a strainer. When at last this was completed the chief's daughter, a very pretty girl with a beautiful white smile and a splendid mop of frizzy black hair carefully combed out in the traditional fashion into a huge globe, came into the ring holding a cup made from the polished shell of a coconut. This was filled by a squeeze from the fibre strainer and then the master of ceremonies called my name. I had been drilled sufficiently by Manu to know that I had then to clap my hands in acknowledgement thus showing the kava server where I was sitting. The girl, stooping, came across and presented the cup to me and I lifted it to my lips. When I had first drunk kava in Suva it had tasted to me rather like gritty mouthwash and I had not cared for it greatly, but I was beginning to appreciate it more and now I positively enjoyed the slightly anaesthetizing sensation it gave to my mouth and lips. I knew that it was important to take only one drink from the cup but I also knew that it was not necessary to drain it, for I had seen some kava drinkers leave the gritty dregs at the bottom and throw them out over their shoulders before returning the cup. However, I decided not to risk this last refinement, as I had the feeling that it might be considered a frill which would not come well from someone as new as I to kava drinking: I might be regarded as being as bumptious as the young sub-lieutenant in a naval wardroom who says 'God Bless Her' after the loyal toast, a remark which, as everyone knows, can only be properly made by officers of the rank of commander and above. I therefore swallowed the entire cupful, dregs and all, but to add a little panache to the proceedings,—I sent the cup spinning back across the pandanus mat towards the bowl with a flick of my wrist, as I had seen Manu do on a previous occasion. This produced grins and a chorus of 'Vinaka, vinaka,' from the villagers at the head of the ring and was obviously interpreted as an indication that we were participating fully in the spirit of the ceremony.

One by one, we all drank, each clapping hollow-palmed after we had been served, as a sign of respect to the kava. When everyone had received his cupful, the formal atmosphere melted a little and people who hitherto had been sitting bolt upright and cross-legged, now relaxed their posture and stretched their legs, some lying on their sides, others resting on their elbows. To me this was an inexpressible relief, for sitting cross-legged becomes extremely painful after a few minutes to someone who is unaccustomed to it. I had remained in this position for the best part of half an hour, not daring to stretch my feet out in case this might offend custom and by now considerable portions of my lower half seemed to have lost all feeling. Stiffly I stretched out my legs, waiting for the sensation to return to them before I attempted to stand up.

A young Fijian came over and sat by me. He introduced himself, in perfect English, as Henry, the village school teacher, and as the kava circulated again he told me the legend associated with the origin of the firewalk.

'In the old days, our people used to gather each evening in one of the mbures to listen to the story-tellers. It was the custom that each man should promise to bring a gift, a *nambu*, to the story-teller the next day. One evening, a young chief named Tui N'kualita promised that he would bring a nambu of an eel.

'The next morning, to keep his word, he went up the creek that flowed behind the village to look for an eel. Soon he came to a muddy pond, just the sort of place where you might find an eel, so he began to dig. After some time he thought he saw something moving in the bottom of the hole that he had dug, so he thrust his hand inside and caught hold of something slippery. He began to pull. Then a voice rang out from the hole saying "Help! Let me go."

' "No," said Tui N'kualita, "I am going to catch you and take you back to my village as a nambu."

' "If you will let me go, I will make you the best navigator in the world."

'Tui N'kualita pulled harder and said, "I *am* the best navigator in the world."

' "If you will let me go, I will make you the best javelin thrower in the world,' pleaded the voice.

' "I *am* already the best javelin thrower in the world. No one can throw it farther than I.'

' "Let me go and I will make you the most handsome man in the world."

' "I *am* the most handsome man in the world. No woman can resist me." '

('He must have been a very talented fellow,' I said to Henry.

'He was a Mbengga man,' Henry replied solemnly.)

' "Let me go," said the voice, "and I will give you the power of walking on fire without being burned."

' "Well," said Tui N'kualita, "that is quite a different matter. Come out of your hole and show me what you mean."

'And out of the hole came not an eel, but a tiny little man, a sort of elf, whose name was Tui na Moliwai.'

('There are a lot of Tui's in this story,' I murmured.

'Well, Tui means chief,' Henry explained, 'and Moliwai was the name of the pool.')

'Then Tui na Moliwai began to make the kind of earth oven that we call a *lovo*. He dug a big pit, filled it with large boulders, piled timbers on top and then set light to them. When the fire had burnt for some hours and the boulders were extremely hot, the elf took Tui N'kualita by the hand and led him four times around the lovo, their bare feet treading on the stones. When they came out they were quite unharmed.

' "Now," said Tui na Moliwai, "you and I must be buried together with the stones in the lovo for four days."

' "I cannot agree to that," replied Tui N'kualita. "You might play some trick on me, and anyway I must be getting back to my village or they will begin worrying about me."

144

' "All right," replied Tui na Moliwai. "Then we must bury ome *masawe* instead." '

('Masawe is a sort of vine,' interjected Manu, 'which when is ripe contains a lot of sugar. We often cook it in lovos and ake it into puddings.')

' "Thank you," said Tui N'kualita. "Now I will release you nd I will find something else for my nambu."

' "Thank you," replied Tui na Moliwai. "From henceforth ne gift of walking on fire shall be yours and your descendants' r ever."

'And ever since then,' concluded Henry, 'the people of 1bengga have had the power of walking unharmed on fire.'

*   *   *

he lovo had been excavated at the back of the village. It as a circular pit some fifteen feet in diameter and four feet eep. Around it lay piles of heavy logs and blackened boulders f stone. That evening, the men of the village began to stack he timbers in the lovo. Many of the logs were so heavy and ulky that two men were needed to shift them. They threw few boulders into the lower layers, but most of them were eaved on to the top of the finished pile, six feet above the round.

Henry explained that the fire must be lit exactly eight ours before the ceremony was due to take place and, as it ad been decided that the performers should enter the pit round noon the next day, it would be set alight some time efore dawn.

We slept that night in the chief's mbure. Henry woke us at hree o'clock and we stumbled through the darkness to the ovo. Three men, holding torches of blazing palm leaf stems, ame down to the lovo and thrust the flames down the side f the pit to reach the small sticks that formed the foundaion of the pile. Soon these caught alight and then, as the lames licked up around the big timbers, the bonfire began to oar. Jets of scarlet sparks spouted upwards towards the yellow moon, and the stones, as they heated, began to split with cracks as loud as pistol shots, fragments of them coming spinning out of the fire to land at our feet. We watched this impressive blaze for some time and then, as the night sky began to bleach with the dawn, we went back to bed.

Five hours later, in mid-morning, we found that the fire was still burning. Most of the timbers had been reduced to

ash and their burden of stones had sunk below the level of th
ground, but there were deep red glows between the flakes o
white powdery wood ash and the pit was still so hot tha
when a few more logs were thrown in they burst into flam
almost immediately.

We seated ourselves on the steep grassy bank at the back o
the lovo and just before noon the ceremony began. A colum
of men, led by the chief and the tribal priest, silently file
towards the pit from the centre of the village. They wer
wearing full traditional costume – long kilts of pandanus lea
strips dyed red, green, and yellow; sashes of black and whit
bark cloth; garlands of flowers around their necks and chap
lets of shredded pandanus leaves in their hair. Their brow
bodies glistened with coconut oil. They walked quietly pas
the pit, keeping their eyes averted from it, for it is forbidde
for any performer to look on the fire before he enters th
lovo. They strode past us towards a small leafy hut standin
beneath a breadfruit tree.

Those men who were merely assistants in the ceremon
continued past the hut, circled and returned towards the lov
but the men who were to walk on fire left the column an
stooped into the hut. The last of them shut the door behin
him.

The tribal priest, an elderly heavily jowled man with bush
greying hair, gave the instructions for the preparation of th
pit. First the unburnt timbers had to be removed. The me
noosed them with loops of vines on the end of poles and then
whooping and cheering, dragged them far away beyond th
trees. Next the jumble of boulders had to be levelled to pro
vide a roughly even surface on which to walk, and this the
did by first placing the trunk of a tree fern across the lovo an
then using it as a fulcrum against which they could use th
poles as levers to shift the huge hot stones. Finally bundles o
freshly-gathered green leaves were placed in a ring aroun
the margin of the lovo. All this had taken some twent
minutes but although the stones must have cooled slightly
there was no doubt whatever that they were still searingl
hot. The air above them shimmered, the heat rising with suc
intensity that it struck you in the face like a physical blo
if you stood within five feet of the edge of the pit. I was qui
certain that under normal circumstances the stones woul
scorch and burn any flesh that touched them.

The men who had prepared the pit squatted around it b

e bundles of leaves. The priest, standing alone, turned to-
ards the hut where the men who were to walk still sat in
arkness and called a single word of command, '*Avuthu.*'
here was a pause. Then the door of the hut opened and the
en, in single file, came running towards the pit at a jog
ot. There was absolute silence except for the rhythmic
vishing of their pandanus kilts. Without any hesitation, the
ader entered the lovo. Slowly, deliberately, his head bent
rward and his eyes upon the stones, he walked round the
it. The other men followed behind him. They did not flinch
om the stones. They did not tread lightly or quickly. They
laced their full weight on every step. It took the leader about
venty paces to complete the circuit of the pit. Suddenly, as
e reached the point at which he had entered, the attendants
rouching in a circle round the lovo, leapt to their feet and
hrew the bundles of leaves into the centre of the pit. The
valkers turned towards the middle, stepped on to the bundles
nd stood in a tight knot, their arms round one another's
ecks, and as the steam from the scorching leaves swirled
ound them, they burst into a droning yet passionate chant.
Two of the helpers dragged into the pit the long brown
nasawe vine that had been lying near by. Frantically the rest
f the attendants began to shovel earth into the pit. The men
rouped in the centre continued their wild song, treading the
oil beneath their feet. Within a few minutes, the stones, the
nasawe vine and the leaves were all buried. Slowly the men
drifted away and soon all that was left was a wide patch of
reshly turned earth from which wisps of steam still rose. The
ceremony would not be complete, however, until four days
ad passed. Then the masawe vine would be dug up and made
nto puddings which all the villagers would eat.

As soon as the men left the pit, I examined their feet.
They were, of course, covered with thick calloused skin, as
are the feet of any people who go barefoot most of their
lives, but even calloused skin will scorch and there was no
sign of any burning whatever. Furthermore, they were not
insensitive for the men flinched from the touch of a lighted
cigarette on the sole.

One of the men who had walked was the local medical
assistant, an educated man who had received his medical
training in Suva. I asked him what he had done in the
twenty minutes he had spent in the darkness of the hut before
the ceremony, expecting to be told that he had prayed or had,

in some way, induced in himself a trance. But he said th
they had done nothing except talk in low voices about t
ritual they were about to perform. Nonetheless, he did s
that when they ran out into the bright sunlight he had felt
though a new strength had come into his body. A man sitti
next to him expressed it slightly differently, saying that
had felt as though a god had entered his belly. A third sa
that everything had looked strange and misty. All of the
agreed that when they walked upon the stones they had e
perienced little sensation of heat and none of pain.

I asked the medical assistant why he had performed t
walk. He did not seem to be very sure. It was not to pro
that he was strong and brave, neither was it because
thought the ceremony might have some purging power. Pe
haps, he said in a pensive objective way, he had done
because no man was truly a Mbengga man until he had pra
tised the strange ability given him by the gods and prove
that the story of Tui na Moliwai was a true one.

I asked him if I too could have walked on the stones wit
out being burnt. He replied I could have done so provide
that I had entered the pit with him and had observed all t
taboos beforehand – that I had not eaten any coconut and ha
remained in a state of purity for the four days preceding t
ceremony.

Many people have witnessed the firewalk. The Mbengg
men have performed it in Suva on several occasions and ha
even gone to New Zealand where they have trodden on t
stones in front of great audiences. Once they did so before
committee of doctors who carried out a scientific examina
tion of the ceremony. Many explanations have been put fo
ward to account for their strange ability. Because the me
insist on taking stones from their own island wherever the
perform, some people have suggested that these boulders a
of a curious stone which possesses the property of losing hea
with great rapidity. But, in fact, the rock proves to be a
andesite, a perfectly normal fine-grained igneous rock whic
retains heat for a very long time. Others have said that t
walkers smear their legs with some solution or ointment whic
protects them from the heat; but no one could produce ar
ointment that has this odd power, and the doctors wh
examined the walkers' feet were unable to find any sign
such treatment. Perhaps the most convincing of all the sug
gested explanations is that the soles of the men's feet produ

148

coating of sweat and that this, combined with the thin cool skin on the outside of the boulders, was sufficient to protect them from harm. For my part, I do not think this explanation is convincing enough. I am quite certain that under normal conditions those stones would have caused the most terrible burns. But they did not. They did not even mark the surface of the skin.

Science has yet to explain many strange happenings in which it would seem that the mind is able to control the body. Hindu holy men pierce their tongues and cheeks with knives without feeling pain or shedding blood; Christian mystics produce unaccountable open wounds resembling the stigmata on their palms and feet; Turkish dervishes in a state of trance thrust spikes into their scalps; and Balinese dancers try to stab themselves with daggers yet fail even to break the skin. All these are well-attested happenings yet none, so far, has been completely accounted for in scientific terms. Perhaps in time to come, physiologists will identify some principle which will enable us to understand how people are sometimes able to endow their flesh with characteristics it does not normally possess and thus explain these extraordinary phenomena and solve, among other things, the mystery of the Mbengga firewalkers' astonishing performance.

CHAPTER FIFTEEN

The Outer Isles of Fiji

NEARLY TWO hundred miles east of Suva, almost midway between Viti Levu and the islands of Tonga, a mountain range rises from the ocean bed, the peaks of which project above the blue waters of the Pacific and form the coral-girt, palm-clad islands of Lau.

Manu and Sitiveni described them to us in rapturous terms. There, they said, the hibiscus and frangipani bloom as nowhere else and the palms produce the sweetest and largest coconuts of the Pacific; the islands have always been the home of the finest craftsmen of Fiji and only there do the old skills of canoe-building and kava bowl-making still survive. And of course, they added, it was universally agreed that the girls of Lau were the most beautiful in the whole of Fiji. Both Manu and Sitiveni, we discovered, came from Lau.

Suspecting that perhaps they were a little prejudiced, w
tried to get corroboration of their claims, but very few peopl
in Suva, who were not in fact Lauans, had ever been to th
islands. Communications were difficult and the only ships tha
made the journey with any regularity were small and ex
tremely uncomfortable trading boats that went out there t
collect copra. Nonetheless, it seemed that Manu's and Sit
veni's eulogies were not entirely without foundation, fo
everyone who had even heard of the islands assured us tha
it was in Lau that the twentieth century had made the lea:
impact and that the old Fijian customs had lingered th
longest. Our minds were finally made up when we learne
from Sitiveni's father, himself by birth a noble of Lau, th:
on the island of Vanua Mbalavu, in the north of the grou;
a strange ceremony was soon due to take place during whic
the sacred fish of an inland lake would rise to the surface an
give themselves up to the villagers.

By good fortune, a government launch was schedule
within the next few days to leave Suva with a surveyor an
take him to Vanua Mbalavu. He was going to assess the po
sibilities of building an airstrip for a New Zealander wh
owned a large coconut plantation in the northern part of th
island. If we wished to see the fishing ceremony, we shoul
have to stay at the village of Lomaloma in the south, but tl
launch could easily leave us there on its way, and fortunatel
there was just enough spare room on board for the four of us.

The voyage took some time, for the crew of the laund
anchored each night in the lee of some island as they wei
unwilling to risk sailing through these heavily reefed wate
in the darkness, but on the evening of our fourth day out, y
entered Lomaloma Bay. We scrambled ashore hastily, for tl
launch had to reach the New Zealander's plantation twel
miles to the north before nightfall. Our baggage was bundle
out of the hold and dumped on the beach, the launch we:
hard astern and steamed away. But we had not been left alon
for dozens of men, women and children had come down to tl
shore to meet the boat and there were many willing helpers
carry our luggage up to the village. Most of the men wl
walked beside us wore not trousers, but sulus, simple lengt
of cloth wrapped around their waists like skirts, some re
some blue, all of them brightly coloured. The girls were al
gaily dressed in cotton frocks and many of them had p
flowers in their hair – scarlet hibiscus, or the elegant ivor

loured blossoms of frangipani. I noticed that whereas all
the people of Mbengga had had frizzy hair, there were
several people here whose hair was wavy and glossy, an
indication of the influence of the Polynesian people of Tonga
away to the east.

Lomaloma proved to be a pretty and very well-kept settlement. Many of its trim thatched mbures were surrounded by
flower beds and between them stretched neatly clipped lawns.
There was a school, two Indian-owned stores, a white-painted
Methodist church and a small radio transmitter operated by
one of the villagers. It has always been an important place.
In the middle of the nineteenth century, the northern Lau
Islands were conquered by one of the greatest of all the
warriors of the Pacific, the Tongan chief, Ma'afu. He made his
headquarters at Lomaloma and established a large Tongan
community there. Even today, one section of the village is
proudly and independently Tongan. Later, after Fiji was ceded
to the British crown, Lomaloma became the residence of the
district Commissioners who ruled over the whole of Lau,
and their office buildings, and the ships' cannon that stood
outside them, still remain. Now, however, the administrative
centre has been moved south to the island of Lakemba, in the
middle of the group. Even so, Lomaloma still retains an air of
dignity and importance which distinguishes it from the more
ramshackle and untidy Fijian villages of other islands, and it is
still the home of the *mbuli,* the government-appointed chief
who is responsible for the administration of the whole of
Vanua Mbalavu. It was he who welcomed us and who was
to be our host throughout our stay. He was a heavily-built
sombre man, deeply respected by the rest of the community.
He seldom smiled and when he did so out of politeness to us,
the expression seemed a painful one and vanished from his
face with almost startling rapidity. He was a 'strong' man, we
were told, and as an example of how he wielded his authority
and backed up his discipline one of the younger men described
an occasion when the mbuli discovered a group of people
making 'home-brew' – the highly alcoholic and illicit drink
that is sometimes secretly made from mandioca, pineapple,
sugar and yeast. He took the culprits out one by one and
thrashed them, and none of these full grown men dared offer
any resistance.

He allocated to us a large beautifully built mbure that stood
in the middle of the village close to his house. Its floor was

covered by several layers of pandanus mats so that it wa
pleasantly springy underfoot and its magnificently constructe
roof, the rafters and cross-stays neatly lashed with sinnet, wa
supported by four free-standing hard-wood columns nearl
two feet in diameter. Normally this splendid building wa
used for community meetings, but now some beds were pu
in it and we were told to consider it our own house.

Although we were the guests of the mbuli, the work o
looking after us fell to his womenfolk. Fortunately, he had a
large number of them – his wife, a fat jolly woman; his cousi
Hola, a thin woman with protruding teeth and a recurren
bubbling laugh who did most of the cooking; and his tw
daughters, Mere (Mary) and Ofa. Mere was nineteen and th
beauty of the village. Her hair was always carefully combe
into the big globe now regrettably abandoned by man
Fijians. She seemed very shy and seldom lifted her eyes fro
the ground when there were men present. Occasionally, how
ever, if someone made a joke, or a saucy remark, she woul
look up and flash a small-toothed brilliant smile which ever
man in the village found very fetching. Ofa was two year
younger and very like Mere, though she lacked her sister
poise and her face often clouded with childish uncertaintie
Hola cooked in a special hut by the mbuli's house and Mer
and Ofa would bring us our meals serving them on a foot-hig
table, covered by an immaculate white cloth. As we at
sitting cross-legged on the floor, the two girls would remai
at either end of the table to brush away with fans any flies tha
might try to settle on the food. The dishes Hola prepared fo
us were delicious – raw fish in coconut milk, boiled chicke
and yams, fish grilled on wooden spits, mandioca, swe
potatoes, bananas, pineapples and ripe juicy mangoes.

Our immediate neighbour was a fat cheerful man who ha
some congenital defect in his speech and was called affec
tionately in the village, Dumb William. But he was far fro
dumb, for although he could not articulate precisely, he pr
duced a wide variety of extremely expressive noises and wit
the aid of swirling, stabbing, waving gestures and frequen
rollings of his eyes he could carry on elaborate and perfectl
comprehensive conversations. Indeed, for us who could n
understand more than a few words of Fijian anyway, he wa
one of the most easily understood of all the villagers. He cam
into our mbure almost every evening and regaled us wit
hysterically funny Rabelaisian stories about our neighbours.

152

William's proudest possession was a battery radio which nce his disability had also made him partly deaf, he played tremely loudly. But he did not listen very much to the radio ogrammes from Suva. The villages up the eastern coast of anua Mbalavu were connected by extremely antiquated lephones that once served Suva and which, when they were utmoded, were sold to the chief of Lau who had them stalled in several of his islands. As there was only one line, inding the handle on the side of one telephone caused every her instrument in the island to ring, so to indicate for whom e call was intended, a kind of Morse code of rings was used. omaloma's telephone was placed in the mbuli's house and l day long it emitted an indecipherable jangle of rings. No e paid much attention or seemed to bother whether the call as intended for Lomaloma or not. Except for William. For m, the whole system provided an endless source of amuse- ent, for he had discovered that by tapping the telephone ire and connecting it to the speaker of his radio set he could ormously amplify the sound and listen to conversations tween all the people of the island. He spent hours sitting by with an absorbed expression on his face and thus became e village's major source of gossip and scandal. Because he ent so much of his evening in our mbure, and because we uld understand his own private language of gurgles and stures almost as well as anyone else could, we rapidly be- me very well informed about the private life of almost eryone in the village. As a result we were not only able to are in scurrilous jokes with our neighbours and acquain- nces but could even improvise a few ourselves. Within a w days we began to feel that we were no longer total rangers, but that we were become quite intimately inte- ated into the community.

The ritual fishing of Lake Masomo, the ceremony which ad drawn us to Vanua Mbalavu in the first place was due to ke place three days after we arrived. Manu told me the gend of its origin, with continual interruptions and graphic nbellishments from William.

'Once upon a time, a man on this island was working in his lantation when he saw two girl-goddesses from Tonga flying verhead. They were on their way to visit a relation who had arried a Fijian man and were taking with them a present of me fish, neatly parcelled up together with water, in a big af of the wild taro plant. The man called up to them that he

was thirsty and asked if they could let him have a drink. The
ignored him and flew on. This made him very angry, so h
cut a branch from a *ngai* tree and hurled it at them. But instea
of hurting them he merely knocked the gift from their hand
The water fell and formed Lake Masomo and the sacred fis
of the gift have lived in it ever since. But they are taboo. N
one is allowed to try and catch them except when the pries
give permission.'

When the day of the ceremony arrived some thirty of u
from Lomaloma climbed aboard the village launch and saile
off northwards to join people in the settlements of Mualev
and Mavana whose priests, by tradition, controlled the rite
They too had their launches, and by mid-morning we were i
the middle of a small northward-bound convoy travellin
between the fringing coral reef and the high limestone clif
that form the coast of this part of Vanua Mbalavu. After tw
or three miles the leading boat turned inwards to the entranc
of a long narrow fjord that snaked deep inland between stee
rock precipices. When at last the water shallowed we wen
ashore and walked for another half-mile first through mudd
mangroves and then up a steep rise. Beyond, we found Lak
Masomo, a black sinister sheet of water no more than thre
hundred yards long, cradled in the hollow of the heavil
forested hills. Some of the men from Mualevu had been work
ing here for several days, felling trees and shrubs to make
clearing by the shore of the lake and building there half
dozen long shelters, simple frameworks of timber thatche
with green leaves. Soon a hundred people had gathered in th
clearing. The women and girls began lighting fires for cook
ing and unpacking the taro and mandioca that they ha
brought with them wrapped up in leaves. Some of the me
went into the bush to cut more branches with which to exten
the shelters. Everyone seemed excited and as light-hearted a
a bank holiday crowd at the seaside.

The rituals began with a series of kava presentations. Firs
we ourselves, as strangers at the ceremony, gave kava to Tu
Kumbutha, the chief of Mavana who was the most senio
chief present. Then the various clans of the three village
presented kava to one another, and finally we all went up to
small shelter set fifty yards away from the rest of the huts t
pay our respects to the head of the priestly clan who governe
the whole ceremony. After he had accepted kava, he pro

ounced that the time was suitable for the rituals to com-
mence.

Immediately, Tui Kumbutha despatched his orator to make
he announcement public.

'Permission has been granted for the fishing to begin,' he
alled, standing in the middle of the clearing.

'Vinaka, vinaka,' we all replied.

'Everyone here must take part. You must enter the waters
of the lake, and, two by two, you must swim. It is forbidden
or anyone to wear any clothing whatsoever except for skirts
of ngai leaves. Anoint your bodies with oil, for otherwise the
waters of the lake will bite you. You must swim until the
priest announces that the time has come to take the fish. Only
hen may you take spears and gather the fish which will rise
o the surface of the waters and give themselves up to you.'

The people needed no encouragement. While the men had
been engaged in the kava ceremonies, the girls had been busy
making heavy skirts from the long glossy leaves of the ngai
ree, a branch of which the man in the legend had hurled at
he flying goddess. The men took the completed skirts and
slung them round their waists and then the girls helped them
to anoint their bare chests and legs with coconut oil deliciously
perfumed with the essence of crushed blossoms, until their
magnificently muscled bodies glistened a golden honey-
brown.

Most of the men had already cut for themselves short logs,
stripped of bark, which were to be used as floats, and holding
them above their heads and whooping with excitement, they
ran down to splash into the lake. Manu and Sitiveni, already
beskirted, came to tell us that both Geoff and I were expected
to help in the ceremony. Unfortunately, Geoff had several
ulcers on his leg which were giving a lot of pain and he decided that it would be unwise to swim, but there was nothing
to prevent me from doing so. Hola had made a skirt for me,
and when I had put it on, Mere oiled me thoroughly. Manu
gave me a log float and we went down to the lake together.

The waters were shallow and extremely warm but the
pleasure of swimming was somewhat marred by the fact
that the bottom was covered with a thick black ooze into
which we sank up to our knees. However, we soon learned to
avoid it, even where the water was only two or three feet
deep, by floating horizontally with our arms resting on our
logs and kicking with our feet. Towards the centre of the lake

the water was deeper and it was possible to swim more actively without becoming covered in mud. Soon, with shrieks and giggles the girls also wearing skirts and their bodies shining with oil, came running down to join us. A few of them brought log floats of their own but most swam over to the men and shared theirs. Then, in a long line, we all swam across the lake singing loudly, kicking out with our feet so that the water behind us swirled black with ooze. Soon the unmistakable smell of sulphuretted hydrogen was rising from the water and, as I smelt it, I understood the way in which the ceremony worked. The gas had been produced by vegetable matter rotting at the bottom of the lake and until we had disturbed the waters, it had lain entrapped in the ooze. As it dissolved in the water, it would form a poison which would force the fish to the surface to 'give themselves up' as the priest had so mysteriously predicted. This also explained why the ritual stipulated that people should oil their bodies, for sulphuretted hydrogen, in solution, forms a weak acid which if it were sufficiently strong, could cause a rash on unprotected skin.

We swam for nearly two hours and then, one by one, we came out and went back to the encampment for an evening meal. But most of us returned as soon as we had eaten. In the cool of the evening, wearing only our skirts of leaves it was warmer in the lake than out of it. A huge yellow moon rose above the mountains and spilled its light in a rippling avenue over the black water. We swam in parties, sometimes losing one another in the darkness and joining other groups, our shouts, laughs and songs echoing over the lake.

After an hour or so, when I was beginning to tire of swimming, I heard, mingling with our own songs, the distant sound of ukeleles and guitars. I waded out and found that back at the camp a *taralala* was in progress. This word derives from the English expression 'tra-la-la' which the dictionary defines as a phrase expressive of joy and gaiety, and its Fijian meaning almost the same, for it is the name given to a happy informal dance. Couples, shoulder to shoulder, their arms around each other's waists, were shuffling back and forth with a simple rhythmic step, in the middle of a large ring of seated people. At one end sat the musicians and singers, and at the other, kava was being mixed and dispensed. The whole scene was lit by the flames of a small bonfire just outside the circle.

'Oi, Tavita,' called the mbuli's wife to me, using the Fijian version of my name by which I was known in the

illage, 'come and show us if you can dance.' I went across
the circle to where Mere was sitting and to the accompani-
ment of whistles and cat-calls from Dumb William, we
aralala-ed with the rest.

We sang and danced and drank kava late into the night.
People came in from the lake to warm themselves by the fire
and to join in the party and then one by one they drifted back
into the darkness to swim again. When I went to my shelter,
the music was still continuing as loudly as ever. I slept for
only a few hours. In the morning, when I returned to the
lake, there were still some twenty people in the water.

During the morning, the fish began to rise in great numbers.
They were huge silver creatures, and as we swam, they
leaped from the surface in front of our noses and flew in a
silver arc through the air before they fell back with a splash.
Many were swimming half-asphyxiated with their mouths on
the surface.

I was floating idly at the end of the lake nearest to the
camp, when I suddenly heard a shout behind me and twenty
men came rushing down the path brandishing fish spears,
long poles with five or six iron spikes radiating from the end.
The priest had given the order for the gathering of the fish to
begin. The men spread out in a line and began systematically to work their way down the lake. The air was thick with
spears. The half poisoned fish, in an attempt to escape, zigzagged wildly across the surface of the water. Some were
already so senseless that the girls were able to seize them by
their tails. Ritual dictated even the small details of the handing of the fish. Normally a Fijian fisherman will thread his
catch on a string which passes through the mouth and out
through the gills, but in this case it was ordained by custom
that the fish should be strung with the cord passing through
their eyes, and all the men had armed themselves with small
wooden skewers in order to do so. Half an hour later, it was
all over. I counted one hundred and thirteen large silver fish
like oversized mackerel lying on the bank. In the evening, we
returned to Lomaloma and that night everyone feasted on
wa, as the fish were called. I thought they were delicious.
Geoff, however, not having taken part in the ceremony, was
perhaps a little less biased, and he maintained that the fish
had the texture of cotton-wool and a taste reminiscent of bad
eggs.

The practical value of the ritual was quite apparent. The

fishing could only be successfully carried out if a large numbe
of people co-operated – and therefore it had to be organized
and its practice had to be carefully restricted for if it we
done too often, the fish might well be exterminated. The mo
convenient way of arranging all this was by turning it into
ritual administered by a priestly clan.

We had arranged before leaving Suva that a small tradir
boat which made a regular tour of the Lau Group shou
collect us from Lomaloma and take us down to the islands
the south, but it was not due to arrive for another week. T.
days which followed the fishing ceremony were among t
happiest and most delightful that we spent during the whc
of our journey in the Pacific. The daily life of the villag
which initially had been disturbed and thrown out of balan
by our arrival, gradually reverted to normal as our presen
came to be taken for granted.

In the mornings, the village woke early. If it was a wee
day, the people would spend their time on community wo
which had been decided upon the previous evening by t
turanga ni Koro, the headman. Perhaps a house had to
built, nets repaired or baskets woven. If it was a Saturda
families would be working on their own account in the
cassava, yam, or taro gardens. If it was a Sunday, no o
would do work of any kind.

We became particular friends of Totoyo, a huge hair
chested man with an incongruously high-pitched voice, w
had the reputation of being one of the best spear-fisherm
in the village. Sometimes we went out with him in his can
and dived together over the reefs. He was a magnifice
swimmer. Wearing tiny goggles that fitted close to his ey
he would dive to fifteen feet in pursuit of a fish, remainir
submerged for minutes at a time.

Once, the turanga ni Koro ordered that a communal fis
drive should be held. The men spent the whole of one d
making a *rau*, a rope of vines several hundred yards lo
around which they twisted the fronds of palm leaves. At hi
tide the next morning, they took it down to the lagoon. Tv
men held one end of the rau on the beach, the rest of it th
piled into the launch. Then as the boat executed a wide circ
in the lagoon, they paid the rau out over the stern. Eventual
the other end was brought back to the beach some fifty yar
away from where they had started. Everyone from the villa
went into the water with it, most of them fully clothed, a

158

stood or swam beside the rau, shaking it up and down. Manu explained that the fronds rattled together and made a loud noise under the water so that the fish did not dare pass through it, but instead fled towards the centre of the circle. Every few minutes, the people on the shore hauled in a few yards of the rau so that the ring grew smaller and smaller. The tide began to ebb and soon shoals of fish could be seen darting back and forth in the shallowing water. We all became very excited, shouting frantically as a shoal swam towards our section of the rau and energetically rattling it up and down in the water. Within an hour, the circle that had been almost a hundred yards across had contracted to no more than five. Then spears were produced and very few of the bigger fish that had been in that patch of the lagoon escaped.

Every evening, as we sat talking after a meal, we received guests. People simply strolled in and seated themselves on the pandanus mats which covered the floor. Sometimes they would bring an object to show us – an old wooden war club, a curious insect, or the flower of a tree we had been asking about; and sometimes a guitar so that they could exchange songs with Sitiveni. Often they came merely to sit, implying that is was not necessary to either sing or talk in order to derive pleasure from a person's company. Dumb William was a constant visitor, squatting in the open doorways flashing a powerful electric torch, which next to his radio was his most valued possession, to see if he could discover some goings-on that could be embroidered into a little bit of scandal. Often, Mere or Totoyo would mix kava and we would all drink.

Outside, the trade winds blew constantly and refreshingly through the rustling palms. The turanga ni Koro walked through the darkened village chanting the list of communal duties that had to be done next day. In the tall mango trees, the huge fruit bats squeaked and quarrelled as they guzzled the succulent fruit, and girls wandered beneath the trees with lamps collecting fallen mangoes, for only at night, when the children are in bed, did enough fruit accumulate to be worth gathering. Other young people would go down to the beach to try and catch land-crabs as they emerged from their holes in the soft turf around the bases of the palm trees.

On these occasions, I often heard a soft bird call, which I could not identify. It sounded neither like an owl nor a nightjar. When I asked Ofa what it was, she hung her head and

159

giggled. Eventually, I discovered from Manu that these were no bird calls, they were the signals of the *moa'uli*.

If a boy wishes to make an appointment with a girl, he does not speak to her himself, but instead persuades one of his friends to act on his behalf – to be a moa'uli, which means roughly 'he who does the dirty work'. The moa'uli goes to the girl and points out to her how talented and handsome his friend is and suggests that the two of them might meet at a particular place and a particular time. If the girl agrees, then the moa'uli does not go and speak directly to his friend as that might be observed and cause gossip. Instead he whistles a signal outside the mbure where the man is sitting to confirm that the arrangement has been made. In this way, many assignations are kept tactfully secret. It seemed to me that from the frequent whistles I heard in the bushes outside and the number of people who were always unobtrusively slipping in and out, that our mbure had become the centre of communications for the young couples of the entire village.

One evening Totoyo brought a small stone adze blade to show us. It was a beautiful thing, smooth to the touch and most elegantly shaped. He said that he had been given it by a man from a hamlet a few miles down the coast who had told him that he had found it in a cave full of skeletons.

The next day, we walked along the beach to the hamlet. Everyone knew of the cave, and one of the men agreed to take us to it. We borrowed two paraffin pressure lamps from the local turanga ni Koro, and together walked up the mountains.

After a mile or so, we came to a sheer limestone cliff. Our guide pointed to a small opening some fifteen feet up. A strangler fig splayed its corded roots over the rock face beneath and provided us with a splendid ladder up which we climbed. We lit the pressure lamps and went inside.

The interior was cold and clammy. Close to the entrance a few ferns and lichens grew in crevices, but beyond the walls and ceilings were draped with stalactites which glittered frostily in the light of our lamps. We picked our way carefully over the rubble-strewn floor. In one place, part of the roof had collapsed and we had to squeeze past a huge jagged boulder which almost completely sealed off the farther recesses of the cave. At last our guide stopped, knelt down and held up his lamp. The cave floor in front of him was strewn with human bones. There were many skulls, some almost perfect, others badly smashed with great parts of the cranium missing. Thigh bones, ribs, and vertebrae lay everywhere in untidy piles. This was no ordered burial ground, for even in the old pagan days the Fijians treated their cemeteries with the greatest respect. It was much more likely that we were looking at a relic of the tribal wars which raged so fiercely throughout the islands until less than a century ago. Often when the war-canoes of a raiding party were sighted, the women and children of a village would flee to the mountains and take refuge in a cave. If their menfolk repelled the raiders, then all was well, but if the attackers were victorious and caught the survivors trapped in a cave, then they were massacred. Only too often such raids had an even more revolting end, for of all the people of the South Seas, the Fijians, a century ago, were the most notorious cannibals.

We turned the bones over gently to see if we could find any clues which might tell us who these people were and how they had died. Beneath a broken skull, I found two small adze blades, one of a hard green stone like the one Totoyo had shown us and the other of what appeared to be ivory, possibly part of a whale's tooth. But they proved nothing, merely suggesting that the bones dated from the time when metal was either unknown or rare. We took the two implements, two skulls and some of the other bones to give to a museum, and left the cave.

As we sat drinking kava in our mbure that evening, we told Totoyo of what we had seen and showed him one of the skulls. He was horrified and gestured wildly to us to take it away. 'Don't let it touch me,' he said. 'Those places are tambu. You should never have disturbed the bones. You will be punished.'

That same evening a messenger arrived from an islet called Susui across the bay. He brought exciting news.

'Tomorrow,' he said, 'the balolo will rise.'

The balolo is a marine worm which lives in tubes in certain parts of the coral reefs, often on the ocean side or by a passage where there is a regular circulation of clean water. At certain times of the year, its hinder end becomes swollen with either eggs or sperms and eventually it breaks off to go wriggling up to the surface of the sea where the sperms and eggs are released. Obviously for this system of reproduction to be successful, it is extremely advantageous that all the worms should perform this action at the same time so that

161

cross fertilization can take place and this, miraculously and inexplicably, is exactly what happens on two days each year. On the first occasion, the rising is comparatively small and often unreliable. The Fijians call it *balolo lei-lei* – the little balolo. A month later, however, comes the day of the great balolo – *balolo levu*. Then the sea over wide areas is full of the wriggling segments and the people go out in their canoes at dawn to scoop it up, for it is considered a great delicacy.

All the travel and natural history books I had read said that the Pacific islanders are able to predict infallibly when the days of the rising will be. But, when we asked in Suva, no one could tell us. Eventually Sitiveni's father decided that a rising would take place during the time we were to spend in Lomaloma. We were delighted. Unfortunately the people in Lomaloma were not so sure. In fact everyone we asked seemed extremely vague about the date. They would have to wait for certain signs, they said, but in any case the next rising would only be balolo lei-lei so it was somewhat unpredictable. Part of the reef around Susui was supposed to be the best place for balolo in the neighbourhood and we had sent a message asking that we should be told when the signs appeared. Now the reply had come. A small patch of the worm had been washed up on the beach that morning. Tomorrow there would be a rising.

The next morning we set off very early, at first light, for the Susui reef. When we reached it, we sat rocking in the boat while the sun came over the horizon and rose into the sky. No worms appeared. Eventually, bitterly disappointed, we returned to Lomaloma. Later that day, one of the villagers came into the mbure and handed me a packet wrapped in a banana leaf. I opened it and inside found a mass of what looked like green vermicelli. 'Balolo,' said the man, grinning. The worms had risen not on Susui, but on another reef some five miles away, and the people, having heard of our interest, had sent us a sample.

'Well, we didn't see the stuff rising,' I said to Geoff, 'but at least we can find out what it tastes like.'

Hola cooked it for us and we ate it that evening. It was very salty and fishy but I thought it excellent. Geoff found it revolting and only ate a small amount.

The next day Geoff's eyelids looked very red and began to puff up. '*Fua-fua*,' said the mbuli's wife. 'Sickness from the sun,' and she anointed his eyelids with a vegetable ointment

162

which he found very soothing. But the following morning, he was very ill indeed. His whole body was covered in angry red weals, his face was so swollen that he could neither open his eyes nor shut his mouth, and he had a high fever. I could only think that he was suffering from a severe allergic reaction to the balolo, similar to the sickness which some people experience after eating strawberries. If this were so, the only cure was anti-histamine but we had none of this highly specialized drug in our medical kit.

One by one, our friends came to the mbure to see Geoff as he lay, mute with pain, his face so swollen that he was barely recognizable. Totoyo was one of the first.

'It was the skulls,' he said to me gravely. 'I told you that you would be punished. They have caused Geoffrey's illness.'

'I too touched the skulls,' I said, 'and I am perfectly well.'

'Do not be so sure, Tavita,' Totoyo replied. 'Your time will come.'

That evening, I sent a cable to Suva describing Geoff's symptoms and asking for diagnosis and advice on what treatment to give him. On the next schedule, I had a reply confirming that it sounded as though he were suffering from some allergic reaction but adding that unless we had anti-histamine tablets, nothing could be done. He would just have to wait until the effects passed off.

The next day, the copra boat that was to have taken us off the island arrived in Lomaloma Bay. It was out of the question to move Geoff. The boat collected its sacks of copra and sailed away without us. Still Geoff showed little signs of recovery. Some of the livid rash faded only to reappear on other parts of his body. I was haunted by the fear that perhaps the diagnosis was not right and that he had some infection that would never get better unless we did something positive to cure it.

For the next two days, I sat by Geoff, bathing his forehead and eyelids which was the only thing we could do which seemed to bring him any relief at all. Hola cooked special meals for him, but he was unable to take any food. One morning we got a cable from our friends in Suva saying that they had discovered that the New Zealander on the plantation in the north of the island had recently received some medical samples which probably included some anti-histamine tablets. Dumb William set off immediately in the launch on the twenty-four-mile journey to see if he could get

them, while I stayed with Geoff. His temperature was sti
alarmingly high and he was still in extreme discomfort. T
our relief, William returned that night with the tablets an
Geoff took a dose straightaway. The very next morning h
temperature was almost normal and many of the weals in h
body had faded.

'Well,' said Totoyo severely, 'it's all right this time, bu
let this be a lesson to you.'

We now had to make new arrangements to leave th
island. It would be a month before another copra boat calle
and the only alternative was to charter a schooner to come o
from Suva to collect us. This we did by radio. The nigh
before it was due to arrive, we held a big kava ceremony
our mbure. Geoff, fully recovered, sat next to me and Mar
and Sitiveni sat on either side of us. At the other end of th
ring sat the mbuli, his wife, Hola, the turanga ni Koro, Dum
William, Totoyo, Mere, Ofa, and all the rest of our friends.

After we had all drunk kava, I walked across the ring an
put in front of each member of the mbuli's family a sma
gift – cloth, perfume, jewellery and knives – which I ha
bought at the Indian store. Then, with Manu translatin
phrase by phrase I made a short speech. I thanked the peop
for their kindness to us, for their hospitality and for the ope
hearted way in which they had received us into their com
munity and said how sorry we were to leave.

When I had finished, the mbuli began to make a speech
reply. He had only spoken a few sentences when unexpec
edly, and in defiance of all custom, his wife interrupted him.

'I must speak. Do not be sad, Tavita and Gefferi,' she sai
with tears running down her cheeks, 'for you can never lea
Lomaloma. Now you are members of our family and we ar
members of yours. No matter where you may go, you wi
take something of Lomaloma with you. And as for us, we wi
not forget you. However long it is before you return her
this mbure is yours to live in for as long as you wish and w
shall always be ready to welcome you back to your secon
home.'

I believed her as I listened. I believe her still.

CHAPTER SIXTEEN

Double Canoes and Turtle Callers

THE NEXT day, a tiny speck appeared on the horizon in the west. Totoyo immediately pronounced it to be the *Maroro*, the ship we had chartered by radio. He could see very little of its shape but from the direction in which it was travelling, the time at which it had appeared, and the shipping news that he overheard daily on Dumb William's blaring radio, he was sure that it could be no other.

Slowly the dot increased in size until at last, through binoculars, we could see that she was a magnificent white-hulled schooner under full sail. Totoyo was right: it was the *Maroro*. Majestically she swung round between the two patches of ruffled water that marked the passage through the fringing reef into the lagoon. When she was no more than a hundred yards from us, she lowered her mainsail and dropped anchor. We said our last farewells and within an hour we had left Lomaloma.

The *Maroro* – her name is a Tahitian word meaning Flying Fish – was captained and part-owned by an Englishman, Stanley Brown, who had come out to the Pacific with the Navy during the war and had been so attracted by the islands that he had settled here for good. He was an ardent and skilful seaman and when he learned that we were two weeks behind our schedule, he suggested immediately that we should sail throughout the night, confident in the accuracy of his navigation to keep us clear of any reefs. As evening drew on, a stiff breeze came up. He stopped the engines, and we sailed on over the starlit sea, the shrouds straining, and the jib creaking, leaving in our wake a broad trail of luminescence.

We made very good speed. During the night we sailed south, past Lakemba, in the centre of the Lau group, and by the afternoon of the next day, we sighted ahead of us our destination, the island of Kambara.

This island is rich in vesi trees, which are only sparsely found elsewhere in Fiji, Tonga, and Samoa and which provide the most prized of all Pacific timbers. Yellow when it is first cut, it darkens with age until it is almost black. It takes a high polish and is so hard that it is virtually indestructible. Even termites avoid it, and it is almost impossible to hammer a nail into it unless you first bore a hole.

From this magnificent wood, the Kambara people produce food platters, combs, log gongs, and above all kava bowls. Indeed, the vast majority of kava bowls in Fiji – and every family has at least one – come from this single island. They also make canoes of several sorts – simple dugouts with out riggers suitable only for paddling in rivers or the calm water of lagoons; more elaborate ones the sides of which are built up with wash-strakes; and a large sea-going version that has a mast and a skeletal platform on the stays between the hull and the outrigger. But the finest of all the creations of the Fijian boatbuilders was the *ndrua,* the great double canoe which was the largest and, in the opinion of many, the finest ocean-going craft ever made by the peoples of the Pacific. Some of the ndrua were over a hundred feet long and were capable of carrying two hundred people for great distances. One was recorded as carrying twelve head of cattle in its holds and Ma'afu, the Tongan warrior chief, converted one of his ndruas into a man o' war by building breastworks of bamboo around the deck and mounting on it a pair of cannon.

The word ndrua means twin, and the basis of these gigantic vessels was two huge dugout canoes each made from several tree trunks skilfully scarf-joined together. These hulls were not in fact identical twins, for one was always smaller than the other. In the centre of the deck stood a hut and by its side rose a mast which supported an enormous triangular sail of mats. A crew of fifty was required to handle them properly and they were steered by paddles, over thirty feet long. The handling of these paddles, even in calm weather, required great strength and in high seas men sometimes so overstrained themselves in attempting to control the oars that they were crippled for life or died during the voyage.

The Tongans also had a type of double canoe, the *tongiaki,* but this was an extremely clumsy craft compared to the ndrua, incapable of tacking and beating to windward. The Tongans, therefore, used to come over to the Lau islands, ally themselves to some Fijian chief, fight for him in the tribal wars and then sail back to Tonga in the ndrua which they took as payment for their services. Others came over and built ndruas for themselves. This was an extremely lengthy business, often taking several years, and as a result Tongan boatbuilders formed an almost permanent settlement on Kambara. Some never left and the Kambara people today have strong blood connections with both Tonga and Samoa.

But the labour involved in keeping an ndrua seaworthy was immense. The pandanus mat sails rotted if they got wet. The sinnet – plaited coconut fibre – which was used as lashing throughout the canoes was subjected to great strains when at sea, and was constantly having to be replaced and this usually involved the virtual dismantling of the entire craft. When European ships began to be seen more commonly in Pacific waters, the Fijians quickly appreciated the advantages of nails and canvas and the new methods of construction. Soon, the building of ndruas was abandoned and the existing ones were allowed to decay. By 1890, there were less than ten in the whole of Fiji and soon afterwards there were none whatever left afloat.

I had asked about these wonderful vessels when I was in Suva, but all that I had been able to see were a few models of them and two gigantic steering oars preserved in the museum. In Lomaloma, the mbuli had shown me a massive timber incorporated in a house that, he said, had once been the corner post of the deck house of Ma'afu's greatest ndrua. When the Tongan had died his boat had been hauled up on the beach at Lomaloma, the capital of his conquered kingdom of Lau, and left there to rot; the corner post was all that remained. Now I was hoping that in addition to filming the Kambara people making kava bowls and small outrigger canoes, we might also find some old man who remembered the last ndruas and who could give us first-hand descriptions of them.

It was not difficult to find carpenters when we went ashore. Every man in the village seemed to be carving something or other. We spent most of the morning watching one of the younger men making a kava bowl. The adzes he used had iron blades but they were shaped like the stone-bladed ones I had seen in Suva museum. To ensure the rim was circular he marked it with a pair of compasses improvised from a length of sinnet and a piece of charcoal, and to scrape smooth the handsomely grained wood he used the curved tusk of a pig.

Later in the day, we found the canoe-makers. They were working among the curving boles of palm trees that grew thickly in the sandy ground above the shore at the far end of the village. With Manu as interpreter, I talked to an old man who sat on his haunches patiently shaping the outside of the hull with an adze. Yes, he remembered the ndruas, but the biggest of them were already rotting when he was a boy and he had never himself sailed in one of the giants. He was rather uncommunicative, answering most of our questions with monosyllables and Manu had to question him laboriously to extract any detailed information about the old boats. I was a little disappointed that he could not give us a vivid impression of a long voyage in an ndrua, but this had been a lot to hope for and I consoled myself with the thought that we had obtained film records of the Kambara craftsmen making kava bowls and dugout canoes, which was in itself sufficient reward for our visit.

That evening we were invited to drink kava with the mbuli. He told us that several of the villagers who owned coconut plantations on the neighbouring uninhabited island of Wanngava had been wanting to go over there to collect some bags of copra. The wind, however, had not been favourable. Could we, perhaps, take them over there in the *Maroro*. The people had been so kind to us that we could not refuse.

The next morning some thirty men and girls came out across the lagoon in canoes and climbed on board. It was clear that the collection of copra was now merely a subsidiary purpose: the trip was really a pleasure cruise. The people sat in the stern, several of them playing guitars and ukeleles, and we sang from the moment that we got under way to the time when the anchor rattled overboard as we lay off Wanngava.

Geoff and I went ashore with the men to look at the island. While I was wandering in the plantations, Manu came to me holding in his hand the largest crab I had ever seen. Almost two feet across, it had a huge heart-shaped body, gigantic claws, and a black fleshy pimpled tail curled up beneath it. In colour its shell was predominantly red-brown but its under side and the joints of its legs were flushed with blue. It was a robber or coconut crab and I handled it with the greatest care for its claws looked quite capable of crushing one of my fingers if I gave them a chance.

Robber crabs are related to our own charming little hermit crabs that crawl around in the rock pools of the British coast dragging their winkle-shell home with them, but these Pacific brutes are so large and armed with such formidable defences that they do not require the protection of a shell-home. Furthermore they have adapted themselves to life on dry land and only need to return to the sea for breeding.

The men told us that the crabs were a great pest in the plantations for they climbed the palms, cut down some of the coconuts and then descended to rip off the husks from the fallen nuts and break them open with their great claws to feast on the soft flesh inside. This is a story which is widespread throughout the Pacific, but one which many naturalists dispute.

I placed Manu's crab on a palm to see if it could climb. Its long legs embraced the rough trunk, their sharp points easily finding holds, and slowly it began to clamber up, moving each of its six legs separately. There was no doubt whatever that it could ascend a palm if it wanted to.

I took it down before it climbed too far and put a piece of coconut in front of it to see if it would eat. The men laughed at me for doing so, saying that the crabs only fed at night. Certainly my specimen refused to take any interest in coconuts, whole or broken, old or newly picked. This, of course, proved nothing, but nevertheless, I found it hard to imagine how the creature, powerful though it was, would manage to split an unbroken coconut for itself.

I showed so much interest in the crab that other people began hunting for them in the holes between the boulders above the shore. Soon we had five of the monsters warily promenading on the soft turf beneath the palms. We watched them with amusement. One of the largest advanced slowly on a slightly smaller one. It reached forward with its pincer. The other crab did the same and the two claws met as if they were shaking hands. For a moment it seemed comic; then it became slightly horrifying. As the aggressor tightened its grip, chips of shell began to fly off the smaller crab's claw with an unpleasant splintering sound. The one that had been attacked brought its free claw forward and with dreadful deliberation fastened it to one of its opponent's walking legs.

We were watching a battle; but it was not one of cut and thrust, of bold dash and cunning parry, but a steady, inexorable tug of war. Only by their desperately waving stalked eyes did the crabs betray any emotion, or give any indication that living sentient beings occupied the huge armoured shells. I was reminded of the eyes of a soldier peeping through the steel slit in the front of a tank. The struggle continued for many minutes. I tried to disentangle the crabs, but picking them up seemed only to make them grip more desperately to one another, and they remained locked in soundless relentless combat. Then suddenly, the larger crab's leg that was gripped by the pincer of the smaller one, broke off high up at the joint close to the body. The raw white wound wept colourless blood. The pincers released their grip on one another and the mutilated crab slowly retreated. The victor walked backwards holding the amputated leg aloft in its pincer. Then it dropped the limb like a mechanical grab emptying its load. The battle was over.

*   *   *

As we sailed back to Kambara, Manu and I found ourselves sitting next to the old canoe-maker we had been talking to the previous day.

'Is Tavita really interested in ndrua?' he asked Manu.

Manu confirmed that I was.

'You know, I have got one myself in the village.'

Manu became very excited. I refused to be jubilant. Too often in the past such dramatic news has proved to be based on a misunderstanding. Perhaps the old man's tenses had got muddled and he was confusing 'have' with 'had'. Or perhaps he was meaning to say that he had got a model of ndrua. Point by point we tried to eliminate all alternative explanations, but the canoe-maker stuck to what he had originally said. Back at the village, hauled up on the beach, he had an ndrua; and what was more, if we were interested and if he could find the necessary rigging, he would take us out in it.

I could hardly wait for the *Maroro* to return. When at last we got back to Kambara, we followed the old man through the village to a beach on the other side we had not visited before. There, dwarfing the other outriggers lying beside it, I saw the twin hulls of an ndrua. It was very far from being the size of the old giants, for it was barely thirty feet long – but nonetheless, it was built on the same lines as the ancient craft with which I was so familiar in models and drawings.

While we examined it in detail, the old man wandered away towards a group of thatched mbures and disappeared. During the next hour, he slowly assembled on the beach, a folded sail of pandanus mats, two fifteen-foot-long steering paddles, a mast, several coils of cordage, two long bamboo poles, and a crowd of rather uninterested onlookers. Under his instructions, we spread out the musty triangular sail and tied the bamboos along its two longer sides. Four of the men rigged the mast, others produced some logs to serve as rollers and, with everybody helping, we managed to push it down the beach to the sparkling blue waters of the lagoon.

Manu, Sitiveni, Geoff, and I scrambled excitedly on board.

170

Six other men joined us. They hoisted the sail so that its peak, formed by the two bamboo yards, pointed downwards and lodged in the bows of the bigger hull. For a moment it flapped. Then the wind filled it, and I felt the huge craft surge forward. The old man stood in the stern, his arm around the handle of the steering paddle.

'Vinaka, vinaka,' I shouted to him.

He grinned broadly in reply.

Already the ndrua was moving with exciting speed. Spray from her bows came flying across the deck and the water swirled white in a trail behind her two sterns. From Manu, I discovered that the old man had often in the past left the island at seven o'clock in the morning and reached Lakemba, fifty miles away, by midday. A fair average speed must therefore be of the order of ten knots and I could easily believe it, for we were already outdistancing one of the *Maroro*'s boats powered by an outboard engine which had tried to follow us.

The old ndruas were so speedy that under certain conditions they could overtake a European sailing ship, and as they often put out from the Fijian islands manned by a hundred warriors, eager for plunder and slaughter, to give chase to passing merchantmen, they were much feared. European captains, however, discovered one way of escaping them. If they sailed on a course so that the wind blew from directly aft, the ndruas were unable to follow, for their sails were so enormous that if they were filled by a stiff stern wind, their bows were forced down and they ran under and sank.

As we sailed out into the open sea it was easy to see how this could happen. It was not a rough day, but beyond the protection of the reef, the water was quite choppy. The open deck on which we sat was not, as on a European ship, some distance above the surface of the sea, but only a foot or so from it and often waves broke over the bows drenching us all.

Two hatches in the deck gave access to the hulls below. We looked down them and saw that they contained water several inches deep. This was scarcely surprising, for the boat had not been to sea for a long time and many of the joints must have been leaking, so as we swept along, the hulls creaking and straining around us, Manu and I stepped into the hatches and began to bail.

Soon we had to turn and beat back towards the shore. Tacking, however, was an extremely tricky and difficult operation. The canoe could not execute a simple turn for the shorter of the two hulls had always to be kept to the windward, its function being that of an outrigger. If it was to the leeward, the leverage from the tall mast would drive the smaller hull beneath the water and the whole craft would capsize. A tack had therefore to be achieved in a quite different fashion. Two of the men clambered into the bows while we were sailing at full speed. The captain stood by the rope suspending the sail from the mast. At a word of command from him, the two men picked up the peak of the sail and ran the full length of the deck with it, to place its point in a notch at the other end. Thus what had been stern became the bows. The captain ran to the other end and picked up the other steering paddle. For a few moments the sail flapped wildly, then at last as she veered, the wind filled it again and off we went on the other tack. It was easy to imagine that when a sail sixty feet long had to be reversed in this way during a high wind, the strength and skill required must have been enormous.

With exhilarating speed we sailed back towards the island. Our voyage had only lasted an hour, but I had seen and experienced enough of the performance of our small ndrua to appreciate the immense courage and skill of the sailors who a hundred years ago had undertaken voyages of several hundred miles across the Pacific, their huge double canoes loaded with perhaps a hundred people and navigating not by charts and sextants but by cloud formations, the wheeling constellations, the flight lines of migrating birds and the accumulated knowledge and skill of some of the bravest and most skilful seamen the world has ever known.

*   *   *

After we left Kambara, we sailed north-westwards towards Koro, a hundred and fifty miles away, the last island we would be able to visit before we had to return to Suva. When we had first arrived in Fiji, and had made arrangements for our journey through the outer islands, we had planned to spend two weeks in Koro for the people of the village of Nathamaki, on the north coast of the island, are said to be able to summon at will from the depths of the ocean a sacred turtle and a great white shark. Such a claim is not unique; people in Samoa, the Gilberts and, within Fiji, in the island of Kandavu, are supposed to be able to do similar things

172

but nonetheless the story seemed an extraordinary one. Our delay in Lomaloma meant that now we would only be able to spend twenty-four hours on Koro, but I was very anxious to do so in the hope that we might, even in this short time, witness the turtle-calling.

At dusk on the next night – a Sunday – we dropped anchor off Nathamaki and we went ashore immediately to make our presentation of kava to the mbuli.

He had been expecting us several weeks before for we had sent word to him from Suva of our projected visit, but even though we were so late he appeared delighted to see us.

'You will surely stay here for at least a week,' he said.

'Unhappily, we cannot,' I replied. 'We must leave for Suva tomorrow night for we have passages booked on a ship to take us to Tonga.'

'*Oia-wa*,' cried the mbuli. 'This is bad. We hoped you would be our guests for many days so that we might do you honour and show you something of our island. And today is Sunday, so we cannot even welcome you with a big party and a taralala for it is forbidden by the church to dance on Sundays.' He looked round the kava ring mournfully and at the girls and the lads who stood clustered around the doorways of the mbure watching us.

'Never mind,' he said brightening. 'I have an idea. We will drink kava for another four hours and then it will be Monday and all the girls will come in and we will dance until the sun comes up.'

With considerable regret, we declined this imaginative suggestion, but we promised to return early the next morning with our cameras so that we might film the turtle ceremony.

The next day dawned badly. The sky was filled with low misty clouds which stretched without a break to the horizon and rain squalls swept across the grey lagoon. We swathed our equipment in waterproofs, and took it ashore in the hope that as the day wore on conditions might improve.

The turanga ni koro, who was going to perform the ritual, was waiting for us in his mbure, resplendent in his ceremonial pandanus kilt and bark cloth sashes.

Even though it was raining, he was anxious to go out and call the turtles. I explained that the weather was too bad to film. He looked extremely disappointed so I suggested that instead he should take us to the place where the ceremony was held so that we might decide where to position our cameras should the rain stop later in the day. He agreed, and together we went out into the drizzle. He led us along the beach and up a steep muddy path.

As we walked we chatted, for he had served in the Army and spoke excellent English.

'I think I will call the turtles anyway,' he said to me, casually.

'Please do not bother,' I replied. 'I only want to see the place.'

He walked on for a few steps.

'I might as well call them,' he said.

'I would rather you didn't. It would be infuriating if they came and we were unable to film them.'

He trudged on up the hill.

'Well I might just as well call them.'

'Don't do it for our sake,' I said. 'If they come this morning, they might not bother to return this afternoon.'

The turanga ni koro laughed. 'They always come,' he said.

By now we were walking along the edge of a high cliff. The rain had stopped temporarily and a shaft of watery sunlight was glinting on the sea below. Suddenly the turanga ni koro ran on ahead, stood on the bluff and began to chant at the top of his voice.

'Tui Naikasi, Tui Naikasi,
God of Nathamaki,
Why lives by the shore of our beautiful island,
Who comes when called by the people of Nathamaki,
Rise to the surface, rise, rise, rise.'

We looked down to the sea five hundred feet below us. There was no sound but the rustle of the wind in the trees and the distant lapping of the waves on the shore far below.

'Tui Naikasi, rise, rise, rise.'

And then I saw a tiny reddish beflippered disc break the surface of the sea.

'Look,' I called excitedly to Geoff pointing with my finger. 'There it is.'

As I spoke the turtle dived and was gone.

'You must never point,' said the turanga ni koro reprovingly. 'That is tambu. If you do so, the turtle will vanish immediately.'

He called again. We waited, searching the sea. Then once more, the turtle rose to the surface. It remained visible for

174

about half a minute, then with a stroke of its fore-flippers, it dived and disappeared. During the next quarter of an hour we saw eight more surfacings. It seemed to me that there were at least three turtles of varying size in the bay below.

As we returned to the village I pondered on what we had seen. Was it so very remarkable? If the bay was particularly attractive to turtles and there were always some cruising there, we should have seen them anyway, for being reptiles, they are compelled to rise to the surface to breathe. This would explain why the turanga ni koro was so anxious to call them, for after all, it would have detracted from the miracle, to say the least, if the turtles had risen without anyone speaking a word.

Back at the village the mbuli entertained us to a splendid lunch of cold chicken, taro and yams. As we ate, sitting cross-legged on the matted floor, the turanga ni koro told us the legend of the turtle-calling.

Many years ago, when Fiji was still uninhabited, three brothers and their families came sailing through the islands in their canoe. As they passed the tiny islet of Mbau, the youngest brother said, 'I like that place. I will live there.' So they set him and his family ashore and the two remaining brothers continued their journey eastwards until they came to Koro. 'This is a beautiful island,' said Tui Naikasi, the eldest of the brothers. 'I shall make this my home,' and he went ashore with his family. The remaining brother sailed on until he reached the island of Taveuni where he settled.

In the fullness of time, Tui Naikasi was blessed with many children and many grandchildren and when he came to die, he called his family around him and said, 'Now I must leave you; but if ever you are in trouble, come to the cliff above the beach where I first landed, call to me and I will appear from the sea to show that I am still watching over you.' Then Tui Naikasi died and his spirit was embodied in a turtle. His wife died soon afterwards and her spirit took the form of a big white shark.

Ever since then, before the people of Nathamaki embarked on a great voyage or their warriors set off on a raid, they would assemble on the cliff to feast and dance and finally to summon their ancestors before them, in the shape of a turtle and a shark, to give themselves courage for the trials to come.

I asked an enormous man who was sitting next to me eating

great quantities of yam, whether he believed the story. He giggled and shook his head.

'Do you often eat turtle meat?' I said, for it is a highly esteemed delicacy in most parts of Fiji.

'Never,' he said. 'For us it is tambu.'

He then told me of a curious event that had happened only a few months previously. Some of the village women, fishing in the lagoon, had accidentally caught a turtle in their nets. They hauled it into their canoe to try and disentangle it, but before they could do so a huge white shark appeared and charged them. They tried to drive it away with blows from their paddles but it refused to be frightened and dashed again and again at the canoe until the women feared that it might capsize them. 'We have caught Tui Naikasi,' one of the women said, 'and the shark, his wife, will not go away until we release him.' As quickly as they could, they freed the turtle from the folds of the net and tipped it back into the water. Immediately it dived and vanished, taking the shark with it.

By the time we had finished our meal, the weather had improved considerably and we decided to make an attempt to film the ceremony. From what we had seen during the morning, it would be extremely difficult to get convincing film of the turtle from the cliff top so instead we went round to the bay by boat and landed on a huge rectangular block of stone standing in the water close to the cliff that the turanga ni koro had told us was Tui Naikasi's home. Ten minutes later, the tiny figure of the turanga ni koro appeared at the cliff top. He waved to us, climbed into a big mango tree and began to call.

'Tui Naikasi, Tui Naikasi. Rise to the surface. Rise, rise.'

'If the turtle comes,' Geoff whispered to me, 'don't for goodness' sake get excited and point at it. Just let me film it, before it disappears.'

'Tui Naikasi. *Vunde, vunde, vunde,*' called the turanga ni koro.

I searched the sea with my binoculars.

'There,' said Manu, his arms resolutely crossed. 'About twenty yards away and a little to the left.'

'Where?' asked Geoff in an anguished whisper. The temptation to point was almost irresistible for I could see it distinctly, its head clear of the water as it gulped in air. Then the purr of the camera told me that Geoff had seen it as well.

176

It lingered for almost a minute drifting lazily. Then there was a swirl and it had gone.

'Okay?' yelled the turanga ni koro.

'Vinaka, vinaka,' we yelled back.

'I call again,' he shouted.

Five minutes later, the turtle reappeared, so close to us that I heard it gasp as it surfaced. As I watched it, Manu pulled my sleeve.

'Look down there,' he said softly, nodding towards the sea close by us. Only ten feet from the boulder on which we stood swam a huge shark clearly visible in the pellucid water, its triangular dorsal fin cutting the surface. Quickly Geoff swung his camera and filmed it as it cruised round the boulder. Three times it passed us. Then with powerful strokes of its long tail it accelerated and swam away towards the centre of the bay where we had last seen the turtle. Although we could no longer see its body we were able to follow its course by its dorsal fin. Then that too sank below the water.

I was very impressed. It might be possible to train both a shark and a turtle to come when called, but to do so one would have to reward the animals with food and this I am sure the people of Nathamaki do not do. Was it then merely a coincidence that both the shark and the turtle appeared when the turanga ni koro called? To answer that properly, we should have had to remain in silence on the cliff top every day for perhaps a week carefully noting the frequency with which sharks appeared in the clear blue waters of the bay and turtles came up to breathe. I was very sorry indeed that we were compelled to leave the island that night.

When we got back to the village, we found to our astonishment that the entire population had changed into ceremonial costume. As we arrived a group of girls ran towards us and hung garlands of frangipani blossoms around our necks. Behind them came the mbuli, grinning happily.

'Welcome back,' he said. 'We have prepared a big show for you, for the people feel you should see all our best dances before you leave.'

This was extremely embarrassing, for it was already late in the afternoon and I had promised Captain Brown that we would be back aboard the *Maroro* well before sundown so that he would be able to negotiate the inshore reefs and reach the open sea before darkness fell. But we could not be so rude as to refuse to watch the entertainment that had been prepared for us.

The mbuli led us to a mat laid out on the grass in front of his mbure. We sat down, then he shouted an order and a group of men and women near by began to sing a rousing chant, accentuating the rhythm with claps in unison. A line of men, their faces blackened, holding spears in their hands, marched on to the grass in front of us and began a perfectly drilled war dance, brandishing their spears and stamping their feet. In the old days the words of the chant were usually a recital of the tribe's battle-honours. These are still sung but the one we listened to was more modern and described the valour of the Fiji regiment which had served with such distinction and glory in Malaya.

As soon as the men had finished, their places were taken by children who performed a spirited club dance, stamping their feet and scowling ferociously in imitation of their elders. Verse followed verse as the children marched up and down, swinging their clubs.

It was now getting quite late and I began to feel that I should have to ask the mbuli if he would excuse us leaving. Then thirty girls, garlanded and their bodies shining with oil, came from one of the mbures and seated themselves cross-legged in a line in front of us. They began a sitting *meke*, singing a delightful song and echoing its words by meaningful gestures of their hands and heads, their bodies swaying.

At last they ended amid great applause and laughter from everyone. I got to my feet, and with Manu's help, I thanked the people as best I could.

'And now,' I ended, 'sadly we must go. *Sa mothe*. Good-bye.'

As I stopped speaking, someone began to sing Isa Lei, the Fijian song of farewell. Within seconds the entire village took up the tune singing with great fervour and in perfect harmony. The melody is a very sentimental one and it had never failed to raise a lump in my throat. Now it seemed more moving than ever, for this was in truth our farewell to Fiji. Everyone clustered round us, adding their garlands to those that already hung round our necks.

We shook hands with the mbuli and the turanga ni koro and then we half walked and were half carried down to the beach. Still singing, the crowd followed us. As we pushed off into the lagoon several of the younger people swam after us.

178

When at last we reached the *Maroro*, the sun was already sinking into the sea in a glory of scarlet. Captain Brown started the engines. Slowly we moved across the lagoon towards the passage through the reef. We could see the people running along the beach to the headland close by which we had to pass, until several hundred of them had assembled on the green hillside. As we drew abreast of them we could hear yet again, the melody of Isa Lei drifting across the water. Captain Brown replied with three hoots on the siren. The *Maroro* swung round, the crew hoisted the mainsail and we headed for the open sea.

CHAPTER SEVENTEEN

Royal Tonga

G E O F F A N D I leaned on the rail of the promenade deck of the ungainly shabby merchant ship that we had boarded in Suva. Rain was beating down from the leaden skies with a depressing unvarying insistence, turning the surface of the sea into hammered pewter. For thirty-six hours we had wallowed our way eastwards through rough seas and heavy rain towards the islands of Tonga. Now the engines had reduced speed and we guessed that we were nearing our destination. Ahead of us we could just distinguish through the driving squalls, a horizontal grey smear that must be Tongatapu, the main island of the Tonga group.

It looked neither inviting nor interesting, but I knew it must be a remarkable place. Its inhabitants, alone among the people of the Pacific, have managed to retain their political independence. They have signed a treaty of friendship with Great Britain, but, unlike the once proudly independent kingdoms of Fiji, Samoa, Tahiti, and Hawaii, they have never been taken over by a foreign power and have remained an autonomous and sovereign state. Tonga is the only member of the Commonwealth other than Great Britain to have a ruling royal family of its own. Its economic affairs are so well managed that there is no national debt and income tax is tiny. Every Tongan youth on reaching the age of sixteen is given eight and a quarter acres of fertile arable land as well as another plot for his house. The islanders have had a free health service for many years and their social system works so well that there has never been any need for either old folks' homes or orphanages. The Tongans have also proved themselves to be among the toughest and most daring sailors in the whole Pacific. They have regularly undertaken extremely lengthy and arduous voyages maintaining contact with islands many hundreds of miles away, and a century ago, under their great leader Ma'afu, they nearly conquered the whole of Fiji and only the intervention of the British prevented them from doing so.

It was several hours before we were able to go ashore. The wind was so strong that the captain would not risk taking his ship alongside the unprotected jetty which constituted the harbour of Nuku'alofa and instead launches from the island came bouncing through the waves to collect us.

We were met by Jim Spillius, the anthropologist who had first written to us suggesting that we should come to Tonga. Standing on the quayside in the rain, he introduced us to Ve'ehala, a Tongan nobleman and Keeper of the Palace Records, with whom I had also corresponded about our visit. Jim drove the three of us along the empty flooded roads, splashing impressively through giant puddles. Eventually he turned into a road lined by elegant modern concrete houses, and stopped. Ve'ehala ran out through the rain, unlocked the door of one of them and beckoned to us to enter.

'This is your home for as long as you are in Tonga,' he said. 'A car is in the garage at your disposal. A cook and a servant will be here to look after you and your food will be sent from the Palace. If there is anything that you lack, you have only to let me know for it to be supplied.'

We spent most of the next three days talking with Ve'ehala, Jim Spillius and his wife, also an anthropologist, about the Royal Kava Ceremony, for it was essential that before we tried to film it, we should understand its significance.

The Royal Kava is the most important and sacred of all the surviving rituals of ancient Tonga and, in its enactment, it summarizes and reaffirms the social structure of the Kingdom. In Tonga, as in all Polynesian societies, ancestry and rank has always been of paramount importance. In some other islands before any ceremony may take place, a nobleman's spokesman will recite a long chant detailing his master's ancestry, which may stretch back to the legendary heroes of the creation, so that everyone shall know his qualification for performing the ritual. Although this custom is not followed in

180

Tonga, lineage and precedence are nonetheless of consuming and vital interest, for nobles of royal blood govern the island, each inheriting with his title a section of the kingdom. But this is not a simple feudal system in which a lord extracts wealth from his serfs. The nobleman himself, though he has many privileges, has many responsibilities to his people and he must administer his villages, apportion land to his young men and often spend a great deal of his time and money in looking after their welfare. But although these titles are hereditary, the Queen must give her approval before a noble is confirmed in his rank and should he be considered unsuitable for the office that should by hereditary right be his, the royal confirmation may be withheld. If it is given, however, then the noble is installed at a Royal Kava Ceremony.

In essence the ritual consists of an act of homage by the nobleman which is witnessed by all the aristocracy of Tonga who sit in a great circle. First elaborate and munificent gifts are made to the Queen on behalf of the noble by his subjects. Then kava is mixed and served to Her Majesty and to every member of the circle. The order in which people are served and their position in the kava ring is governed by their lineage. But the determination of seniority and relative rank can be very complicated when aristocracy from all the islands of the group assemble, for nobility is transmitted by both the male and the female line, and temporary non-inheritable positions conferred by the Queen can confuse the position still further. But it is vital that there should be no mistakes, for in the kava ring relative ranks are made apparent to all and in time to come questions of important protocol may well be settled by reference to the last ceremony. It was for this reason that the Queen wished the entire ritual to be recorded on film.

The more we heard about it, the more I realized that the task of filming would be considerably more complicated than I had imagined. The ceremony itself would last over four hours. The kava ring would be a hundred yards across and except in the early stages we should not be allowed to step inside the circle. Furthermore during the most important and sacred parts it would be unthinkable that we should move about, even outside the circle, as we should certainly deeply offend some of the older chiefs who in any case were somewhat suspicious of the whole project. In spite of this restriction of movement, it was vital that we should secure detailed close-up pictures of happenings at both sides of the ring and make recordings throughout the ceremony.

For all this to be achieved, we had to make detailed plans as to where we should place our cameras and microphones, when we should hurriedly move into new positions and, on the occasions when several things were happening simultaneously, which action should be filmed and which ignored. Furthermore, in order to put these plans into action, we should have to be able to follow every intricate detail of the four-hour ceremony which would be carried out in a language of which, so far, we knew not a word.

Jim and Elizabeth Spillius and Ve'ehala did their best to explain it all to us, but their task was extremely difficult for the whole ceremony was in reality a mosaic, each part of which was the responsibility of one noble or officer who was the authority on its protocol. As a result, not even Ve'ehala, keen student of Tongan ritual though he was, could give a definite description of the entire ritual. There was, however, an ultimate authority on these questions, the Queen herself, and after each of our protracted meetings Ve'ehala would return to the Palace and seek an audience with the Queen so that he might be given answers to a long list of problems.

Ve'ehala coped with these trying problems magnificently. He was a young man, short and stout with a round face, and, mercifully, an extremely well-developed sense of humour. His laugh was memorable. It began as a giggle which gradually increased in intensity until his whole body was shaking and then, as he ran out of breath and was forced to inhale, it changed into a startling falsetto squeak.

Like nearly everyone else, he habitually wore Tongan national dress – a neck-tight tunic, a *vala*, the simple skirt like a Fijian sulu, and around his waist, belted with a long length of sinnet, a large mat of woven pandanus leaf strips, the *ta'ovala*. Ta'ovalas can vary enormously in size and quality according to the occasion. For an important ceremony, the mat might be a precious heirloom, extremely old, rich brown in colour and as finely woven and as pliable as linen. At funerals a rough tattered coarsely-woven one would be appropriate. Ve'ehala, I suspect, had as many mats as an elegantly dressed Englishman has ties, but he usually appeared in comparatively new stiff ones which stretched from well below his knees to the middle of his chest. When sitting cross-legged on the ground, such a ta'ovala was obviously extremely

182

useful, providing the wearer with a cushion on which to sit as well as an extended pocket in front of the chest where cigarettes, notebooks, and pencils could be kept, but Ve'ehala found it something of an encumbrance when he had to sit on a chair around a table. Consequently, when we got to know him better he would sometimes take it off, and this he did not by untying the sinnet belt and unwinding the whole mat, but by taking a deep breath so that the mat slipped to the ground and then, gathering his vala around his knees, stepping out of it, leaving an empty tube standing by itself on the floor.

Ve'ehala became the closest of our Tongan friends. He not only looked after our everyday wants, but he spent hours of his time telling us about Tongan legends and history. He was also an expert on the island's music and dancing, and a noted performer on the Tongan nose-flute.

For the first few days, our time was monopolized by preparations for filming and we seldom left Nuku'alofa. It was a sunny unhurried town laid out on a neat but wearisome rectangular grid plan along the shore of a wide bay. The majority of its buildings were modern like the villa in which we lived, but almost as many had been built on traditional lines and were surrounded by kava and mandioca bushes. Apart from bicycles, the streets were almost free of traffic and the few cars that hooted their way through the crowds strolling idly down the middle of the roads belonged either to a Tongan Government official or a member of the small European community. Physically, the people were quite dissimilar from the Fijians of Viti Levu, for they were not Melanesians but Polynesians, tall and handsome with honey-coloured skins, flashing teeth, narrow noses and wavy black hair. Many of them walked barefoot and most wore valas and ta'ovalas, the only conspicuous exception being the girls of Queen Salote's School who were smartly dressed in immaculate bright blue tunics and straw hats that would have done great credit to the most fashionable English Ladies' College.

The focal point of the town is the Palace, a white-painted timber building standing on the shores of the bay, that was erected nearly a hundred years ago by a New Zealand firm. It has two storeys, a feature which in itself is enough to give the building distinction in Nuku'alofa, and though its design is simple, it is ornamented with fretted edgings along the gables and eaves of its verandas which prevent it from appearing austere. It is the home not only of the Queen but of her son Prince Tungi, who is Prime Minister, and his family, and a great number of maids, musicians, dancers, cooks, and servants live in separate buildings at the back. In one of its rooms, Privy Council is held, and on a side veranda kava is almost always being served to visiting notables. Processions of people bearing tapa cloth, fine mats, garlands, roast pigs, and other gifts for the Queen are continually visiting it, and from its kitchens comes the most exciting and reliable gossip in town. In the gardens, watched over by the burly Tongan policemen in khaki valas and bushranger hats who keep formal guard over the Palace gates, wanders another famous occupant, Tui Malilo.

Tui Malilo is a tortoise and, reputedly, the oldest living creature in the world. According to tradition, he and a female tortoise were presented to a Tongan chief, Sioeli Pangia, by Captain Cook in either 1773 or 1777. The chief later gave them to the daughter of the Tui Tonga. After sixty years, the female died and Tui Malilo went to live in the village of Malilo which gave him his name. Finally he came to Nuku'a-lofa.

If the story is true, he must be at least 183 years old, exceeding in age another famous tortoise which was brought from the Seychelles to Mauritius in 1766 and which survived until 1918 when it fell through a gun emplacement. Unfortunately, however, Cook does not mention making such a gift in his journals, and even if he did present a tortoise there is no way of proving that Tui Malilo is the identical animal. It may be that he was brought to Tonga at a later date by some other vessel, for sailing ships often carried tortoises on board as a ready and convenient supply of fresh meat.

However this may be, Tui Malilo is now extremely old. His shell is battered and dented by a series of accidents that have befallen him during his long life – he was trodden on by a horse, trapped in a bush fire and half crushed beneath a blazing log, and for many years past he has been totally blind. The loss of his sight prevents him from being able to forage for himself, so every day someone from the Palace brings him ripe paw-paw and boiled mandioca. Much of the work in the Palace gardens is undertaken by convicts, and this particular job was often carried out by a large and extremely amiable murderer.

Tui Malilo is not the only semi-sacred animal in Tonga. Several miles from the Palace, in the little village of Kolovai, we saw a flock of fruit bats which no one except members of the royal family are allowed to touch.

They hung in enormous numbers from the upper branches of a group of casuarina trees in the middle of the village, large furry brown creatures with protuberant black eyes and dog-like muzzles, their black skinny wings wrapped around their shoulders. Beneath them the ground was befouled with their droppings and the air was loud with their bad tempered squeals and yells. Ve'ehala assured us that they were excellent to eat and it was only because they were protected by custom that they dared to hang so low in such an easily accessible spot. He also told us the legend of their origin.

Once upon a time a Tongan named Ula sailed over to Samoa to take part in the canoe races. While he was there, a Samoan princess fell in love with him and when the time came for him to leave, she gave him some bats as a parting present. Among them was a single pure white one. When Ula returned to Tonga, the bats settled very happily in a tree by his house on the coast.

One day Ula went to visit the chief of Kolovai. The chief said he would like to have the bats himself and as, according to Tongan custom, a commoner cannot deny a high-born man anything he demands, Ula brought the bats to Kolovai and gave them to the chief. The single white bat, however, would not stay with the rest of the flock and followed Ula back to his home on the coast. The remainder stayed in Kolovai where their descendants live to this day. The white one is said to reappear from time to time, but when it does so, it is a sign that the chief of Kolovai or a member of the Tongan royal family is about to die.

Tongatapu is not a large island and there was no village that we could not reach by car from Ndku'alofu within forty minutes. It is very flat and low-lying and the only obvious elevations are a few small conical hills some twenty feet high. I found these very difficult to account for in geological terms. Eventually I discovered that they are not natural mounds at all but man-made and were once used in the ancient Tongan sport of pigeon catching. Eight or nine men used to conceal themselves in small hides on the hill holding nets on the end of twelve-foot rods. Wild pigeons were attracted to the hill by the calls of tame decoy birds tied on long strings and as they flew past they were netted by what an old account describes as 'the dextrous management of the sportsmen'. Today the mounds are overgrown by palms and their original purpose forgotten by many of the people.

The island is extremely fertile. Much of it is covered by plantations of coconuts, the regularity of the rows in which they were originally planted disguised by their swerving grey trunks. But everything seemed to grow in abundance. The people cultivate some twenty different sorts of breadfruit. Taro grows luxuriantly, producing gigantic glossy leaves shaped like those of English arum to which it is related. The villages were not particularly tidy or well kept, but they never seemed squalid as African villages so often do, for the grass grew richly green between the huts, and flowering trees and shrubs blossomed in profusion. Everywhere hedges of hibiscus flaunted trumpets of blazing scarlet with pistils loaded with yellow pollen, and frangipani trees were almost as common, their bloated finger-like twigs sometimes bare but more often exploding into a spray of fragrant blossom.

Scenically, the most beautiful part of the island is the south-eastern coast. It seems that the whole of Tongatapu has been tilted, the northern side having sunk and the southern risen. As a result, the ancient limestone cliffs of the south are now some distance inland beyond the reach of the sea, and the rock platform, that the waves once cut at their foot beneath the surface of the sea, is now exposed above the level of the water. The Pacific rollers that crash on to this side of Tonga break against the outer edge of the platform and have eroded a series of pipes in the joints of the limestone. As each breaker surges in, these blowholes spout plumes of spray twenty feet high with a whistling roar, and water cascades into the shallow lagoons on the top of this platform. The spouting seawater is forced through the pipes at such pressure that it dissolves some of the limestone and this is later deposited to form a series of small terraces around the nozzles of the blowholes. The sight of the whole coast smoking when heavy seas are running and the feathery jets tumbling into the miraculously clear blue lagoons is extremely spectacular and the Tongans, who take a positive pleasure in scenes of natural beauty, often come down to the coast to hold feasts and watch the thundering blowholes.

Ve'ehala took us down there with Vaea, the nobleman in whose territory the blowholes lie, and gave us a feast. Together with some of the senior men of the nearby village of Houma, we sat in the shade of a few pandanus trees that formed a little thicket on the bare coral rock, and the women from the village brought us *polas* for the feast. Each pola consisted of a frame of plaited coconut leaves about six feet long in the middle of which lay a small roast sucking pig, flanked by two chickens, boiled yams, mandioca, sweet potato, red slices of water melon, bananas, boiled Tongan puddings, and young husked coconuts full of sweet cool milk. Garlands were hung around our necks and a group of musicians sang to us as we feasted, accompanying themselves on guitars and ukeleles.

After we had eaten, we went up into the village to watch the making of tapa cloth. Bark is first stripped from the thin stems of the paper mulberry tree and soaked for several days. Then the rough outer layer is torn away leaving only the white pliable inner cortex, and women, sitting in a line behind a log with a specially flattened surface, beat the strips with square-headed mallets. Each end of the log is slightly raised above the ground so that as it is struck it rings clear and an energetic team of tapa beaters produces a quick rhythmic tattoo of high-pitched notes which is one of the most common and characteristic sounds of a Tongan village. Beneath the blows of the mallet, the original three-inch strip soon quadruples its width. As it broadens, so it thins. Then it is doubled and folded and beaten again until it has become a gauzy cream-coloured sheet eighteen inches wide and over two feet long.

When a woman has accumulated several hundred of these sheets, she invites her friends to help her make the final cloth. They use a long bench with a curved top on which are placed patterns made of creepers sewn on to dried palm leaves. The sheets of tapa are laid on top, three or four layers thick and stuck together with smears of a glutinous boiled root. Then they are rubbed with a cloth soaked in a brown dye so that the design from the patterns beneath appears on the cloth.

The finished tapa may be as much as fifty yards long with a bold and handsome design in richly varied russet brown, sometimes outlined later with black. It is used for skirts and for wall hangings, for sashes and for bedding, a single sheet of it being warmer than a thick woollen blanket. It is exported to Fiji where it is regarded as being much superior to the Fijian-made material, and it is used for ceremonial gifts, particularly in offerings that are made to the Queen.

* * *

At last the day of the Royal Kava Ceremony arrived. It was to be held on the *mala'e*, the ceremonial ground adjoining the Palace on the shores of the bay that is Nuku'alofa's equivalent of London's Horse Guards Parade. Geoff, Jim, and I went down there in the early morning with all our equipment. On the side nearest the palace in the shade of a line of magnificent Norfolk Island pines, a small thatched pavilion had been built which would be occupied by Queen Salote. As we arrived its floor was being covered by layer upon layer of tapa cloth.

Ve'ehala, carrying a staff and wearing an ancient and voluminous mat around his waist, appeared soon after. Then, one by one, the aristocracy of Tonga appeared on the mala'e. There were nobles from the island of Ha'apai, a hundred miles away to the north, and from Vava'u, yet another hundred miles beyond. Many were old men with close-cropped grey hair and deeply lined faces. Each was accompanied by his *mata'pule*, his squire or spokesman. Not for very many years had so many attended at one ceremony, but the Queen had let it be known that the record must be complete and no one had failed to appear. If it had not been for the fact that the positions in the circle had been the subject of great discussion for weeks past there would doubtless have been many heated arguments about the seating. Even so, Ve'ehala was called upon to adjudicate on a number of occasions. At the far end of the ring, opposite the Royal Pavilion, shrouded by leaves lest it crack in the sun, lay a gigantic kava bowl, almost five feet across, its surface coated with a thin film of pearly white enamel deposited over many years by the kava that had been mixed in it. The vesi wood of which it was made had come from Kambara. Behind it clustered the *to'a*, people from the village whose noble was being installed.

Posted at the far end of the mala'e stood several policemen to turn away anyone who was not entitled to see the ceremony. Only the Spilliuses, Geoff, and I of the European community had been granted permission to watch and it is likely that we were the first ever to have been given the privilege.

At last the circle was complete, arcing round from the pavilion to the kava bowl, nearly a hundred yards in diameter. The Queen alone was absent. Then the ceremony began. The people from the to'a brought the ceremonial gifts into the centre of the ring. The types of gift, though not the quantity of each, were specified by ritual. There were two gigantic

188

tapa cloths, several hundred coconut leaf baskets some full of mandioca, some of fish, and some of chicken. Roast pigs were brought in whole, with their livers skewered to their chests. There were several different sizes, each with its own name, each with its distinctive type of preparation. The largest of all, the *puaka toko*, was hauled in on a platform of poles, the men singing an impressive tuneful chant. Lastly came the kava bushes, the largest of all, the *kava toko*, also being hauled in accompanied by chants.

When all the offerings had been assembled in lines in the ring, they were counted, men from the to'a lifting each up in turn, for it was important that all should know how much of each type of gift had been subscribed by the noble's people. All the members of the ring chanted thanks for the gifts. The counters retired to the to'a and silence fell. The stage was now set for the arrival of the Queen.

She appeared from the Palace gardens, a truly regal figure, tall and statuesque, wearing a ta'ovala over five hundred years old and a wide thick sinnet belt.

The ceremony now became extremely sacred, tapu. First, one of the roast pigs was presented to her. With swift strokes of the knife, the carcass was dismembered and special parts of it were taken to particular nobles. Some were entitled to eat their share immediately, others were not permitted to do so. The Queen received the regal allotment of the liver. The kava toko was next taken down to the kava bowl where it was broken into pieces, and one section of it pounded. At a command from an official, Motu'apuaka, sitting outside the pavilion, all the offerings were then removed from the ring. With slow hieratic gestures, the man sitting behind the bowl began to prepare the kava. Water was poured into the crushed root from hollow coconuts, and then using a large bundle of white hibiscus fibres as a strainer he began the mixing. His actions were stylized and exaggerated, for all in the kava ring must see that the correct movements were being employed. Again and again he bent forward, gathered the fragments of root in the strainer and then lifted them to twist and squeeze the fibres around his arm.

At last the mixing was completed. At a call from Motu'apuaka, a coconut cupful was taken to the Queen. She lifted it to her lips. Then, one after another for the next hour and a half, everyone drank in the prescribed order. When the last had been served, the Queen stood up and walked

189

slowly back to the Palace. The Royal Kava Ceremony was over.

It had had none of the spectacular qualities of the Pentecost jump or the Fijian firewalking, yet curiously it had been more impressive. Whereas the earlier ceremonies we had seen had been athletic feats, in this, the atmosphere had been sacramental and very moving.

*　　*　　*

The time for our departure was now rapidly approaching. We spent our last days wandering through the villages and along the coast trying to record on film something of the island's magic that had captured both Geoff and me. It seemed impossible. The more we filmed the waving palm trees, the sparkling lagoon and the thatched huts, the more we realized that Tonga's special quality came not from the island, for we had filmed others that were more picturesquely beautiful, but from the people themselves. They were hard-working, devoted to their Queen, and passionate in their attachment to the Church, but their overwhelming characteristic was contentment. In repose their faces always relaxed into a smile – a marked contrast from the furrowed foreheads and set mouths that had characterized the New Hebrideans. But happiness and contentment are not easy things to capture on celluloid.

One evening, we came home late and tired from filming all day in the blazing sun by the blowholes at Houma. As I entered our front door, I thought for a moment that we had come to the wrong house, for our living-room was unrecognizable. Chains of hibiscus blossom hung from the walls and across the windows. A huge spray of cannas filled one corner and the mat-covered floor had been cleared except for the table which had been pushed to one side and loaded with pineapples, bananas, water melons and roast chickens. As I stood, dusty and astonished, staring in the doorway, a young man from the Palace emerged from the kitchen wearing a brightly coloured vala and a flower behind his ear.

'Her Majesty understands that you have had a hard day's work,' he said. 'She has decided therefore that you should have a party.'

Behind me I heard an unmistakable high-pitched giggle. I turned and saw Ve'ehala resplendent in an enormous ta'ovala, quaking with delighted laughter. The music of guitars came from the room in front and a line of Palace dancing girls, grass-skirted and garlanded, advanced from the kitchen, singing as they came. Ve'ehala pushed us in through the door. Vaea was already there and within the next few minutes many more of our Tongan friends arrived. Soon the room was filled with singing, dancing, laughing people. It was past two o'clock in the morning before the last of them left us.

Had we found the people of Paradise? Few of the Europeans we met in Nuku'alofa would have said so. To them the island was a backwater where nothing ever happened and they were bored. Ships only called at very long intervals so that you could not always get exactly what you wanted in the island's few shops and post from the outside world was often intolerably delayed. But perhaps their reactions were understandable, for they had come to Tonga to deal with matters that were quite foreign to the island's life – with electricity and the telephone service, with engineering and commerce – and they were the prisoners of their own professions, endeavouring to work as though they were part of an industrial community, when in fact they were living among a people to whom time, schedules, ledgers and the double entry system of accountancy seemed to be among the least important things in life.

But I am sure that to the Tongans themselves their island seemed the nearest approximation to Paradise that can be found on earth. It is very fertile; there are always fish to be caught in the lagoon; each man has a plot of land of his own and can never starve. Life, indeed, is abundantly good. Flowers are beautiful, food sweet-tasting, girls pretty, and music beguiling. The day has its duties but they are not so demanding that there is not ample time to enjoy its many pleasures.

Perhaps if I had stayed longer, I, like the other Europeans in the island, would have become discontented. I longed to find out.

THESE ARE PAN BOOKS

David Attenborough

ZOO QUEST FOR A DRAGON

TV's famous zoologist recalls an enchanted journey through the islands of Indonesia – Bali, Java, Borneo, and finally Komodo, the remote island where he at last caged the awesome dragon, the largest lizard in the world. This exciting account is David Attenborough at his liveliest. *Illustrated.* (2/6)

Gavin Maxwell

RING OF BRIGHT WATER

The bewitching bestselling account of life with two otter pets. 'Surely one of the most appealing accounts of animal–human relationships ever written. I read it with sheer delight' – Rachel Carson, author of *The Sea Around Us*. *Illustrated.* (5/-)

PICK OF THE PAPERBACKS